Top[...]
NA[...]
Ma[...]
15-[...]
the[...]
NA[...]
ope[...]
nations participate.
The Most Excellent Order of the British Empire. *Founded by George V in 1917, the OBE marks distinguished service in all walks of life, including, for the services, on operations.*
NATO Medal – Kosovo. *For those who served in Kosovo, particularly the 1999 British-led intervention.*
UN Medal – Cyprus. *For those who have served with UN forces in Cyprus since the 1974 war.*
Western European Union Mission Service Medal. *For those who have served in Western European Union-led missions, such as those in the Balkans and the Middle East.*
General Service Medal (GSM 1918–62). *For general service with the British forces on 17 operations short of full scale war between those dates.*
Northern Ireland Home Service Medal. *For those who live in Northern Ireland and have served for 12 years with the security forces there. Primarily awarded to the Ulster Defence Regiment and the Royal Irish Regiment.*
UN Iraq–Kuwait Observation Mission Medal. *For service in the mission that monitored the demilitarised zone along the Kuwaiti border with Iraq, 1991–93.*
UN Bosnia Medal. *For service with the UN-led force in Bosnia.*
UN Assistance Mission in Rwanda Medal. *Only awarded to a few British service personnel who served with the Rwanda mission, 1993–96.*

Bottom row, left to right:
NATO Medal – Former Yugoslavia. *This 1992 NATO operation was the first time NATO had led operations since its inception. In 1994 the first NATO medal was issued for those who served there under NATO command.*
Military Cross (MC). *Created in 1914, and awarded for exemplary gallantry on operations against the enemy on land. Originally restricted to officers, since 1993 it has been awarded to all ranks.*
Operational Service Medal – Operations in Sierra Leone (2000–02). *For those who served in this operation to protect the country from civil war.*
General Service Medal (1962–to date). *Awarded for service on 13 operations short of full scale war since 1962, most commonly for Northern Ireland.*
Accumulated Campaign Service Medal. *For those who have spent over 1,080 days on campaign.*
Accumulated Campaign Service Medal – 2011. *For those who have spent continuous periods (24 months) on operations during a very demanding period for the Armed Forces.*
Queen Elizabeth II Diamond Jubilee 2012 Medal. *To recognise those serving at the time of Her Majesty's Diamond Jubilee.*
Queen Elizabeth II Golden Jubilee 2002 Medal. *To recognise those serving at the time of Her Majesty's Silver Jubilee.*
Army Long Service and Good Conduct Medal. *For completion of 15 years' distinguished service.*
Operational Service Medal – Operations in Afghanistan. *For service in Afghanistan since 2001.*
Iraq Medal – Operation Telic. *For service in Iraq.*
Household Division Ribbon. *Worn by Household Division regiments both behind their cap star or cap badge, and on their right sleeve as a tactical recognition flash.*

The medal ribbons, tailor's shop at Knightsbridge.

THE QUEEN'S
BIRTHDAY PARADE

TROOPING THE COLOUR

Written by

*Major General
Alastair Bruce*

*Major General
Sir Sebastian Roberts*

*Lieutenant General
Sir Evelyn Webb-Carter*

*Lieutenant General
Sir Barney White-Spunner*

*Lieutenant Colonel
the Reverend Bill Beaver*

Major Roly Spiller

*Previous Page:
Coldstream Guards
Ensign with the
Queen's Colour*

THE QUEEN'S BIRTHDAY PARADE

TROOPING THE COLOUR

REVISED EDITION

Julian Calder ✸ Mark Pigott ✸ Alastair Bruce

Jcp

Julian Calder Publishing

Photographed & Conceived
by Julian Calder MStJ

This book has been updated and reprinted since the first edition sold out.

I have spent eight years taking the photographs contained in **The Queen's Birthday Parade**, but this book has been many more years in the making, reflecting my long admiration for the parade and its people.

One might think of Trooping the Colour as a timeless event, fixed in tradition, but over the period of taking these images I have come to appreciate that every year it evolves, changing to reflect the latest practice and sensibilities. The book spans the appointments of four Major Generals Commanding the Household Division, who have ultimate oversight for the parade, and two Garrison Sergeant Majors, who are responsible for delivering the event on Horse Guards parade ground. Each has left their own mark on Trooping. Modern

communication methods also shape each year's parade, as section leaders scrutinise rehearsal footage on their smartphones to provide instant feedback.

The Queen's Birthday Parade is the ultimate photographic subject – it encompasses reportage, controlled portraiture and lucky pictures. But once I came to know it intimately, I discovered even more interesting elements to capture that reflect Britain's fascinating military, ceremonial and royal history.

There is a tangible energy to this event, with over 1,400 soldiers all working hard to make it the best it can be. The Household Division strives to achieve excellence, and it has been a privilege to have witnessed this and recorded some of it.

My warmest thanks go to Sir Mark Pigott without whom **The Queen's**

Birthday Parade and this updated, reprinted edition could not have been published.

I delayed the printing of this revised edition because of Covid-19 and the many problems it has caused. Even as the United Kingdom went into 'lockdown' in March, the Household Division always hoped that some kind of ceremony could take place to celebrate Her Majesty The Queen's Official Birthday. And so on 13th June 2020 a company of the 1st Battalion Welsh Guards, accompanied by the Foot Guards band, trooped their Colour in front of Her Majesty in the Quadrangle of Windsor Castle, while observing the strictures of social distancing.

My thanks to all those who gave up their time to be photographed and to all those who arranged and organised for me to take the pictures.

CONTENTS

HOUSEHOLD DIVISION CHARITY The Household Division Charity funds a wide range of projects which help serving and retired Guardsmen from all regiments of the division and their families. Its formal objectives are to promote the military efficiency, welfare, education and memorialisation of the Household Division, which allow the Trustees, of whom the Major General is the chairman, to support a variety of projects which improve the lives of the Household Division community each year.

Funds are allocated to provide much needed facilities for our injured soldiers or elderly veterans, to promote gatherings for our bereaved families and their supporters, to enhance training expeditions for our soldiers, and to enable many other events at which different groups within our community can meet and reinforce friendships.

The funds support our *Guards Magazine*, our museums, the creation and maintenance of our memorials, and events at which our soldiers can share the long history of our regiments and improve their understanding of the lives and experiences of their predecessors. Most recently the charity has funded the development of our website – www.householddivision.org.uk – where all-comers can find information on the Household Division, its seven regiments and the wide range of parades and events that occur throughout the ceremonial season.

A percentage of the profits from sales of this book will go to the Household Division Charity.

© Crown Copyright

BUCKINGHAM PALACE.

All major battles inevitably become chaotic. The noise of weapons, smoke, dust, and flying fragments of all kinds are bound to cause confusion and disorientation. Battles are won by the army which retains its cohesion and when every man is instantly obedient to orders. This can only be achieved by rigid discipline and frequent practice. The preparation for battle begins on the parade ground.

The Queen's Birthday Parade demonstrates the highest level of military skill. The drills executed during the parade may look archaic, but the need for immediate response to commands and coordination between individuals is as vital as ever, and can only be achieved by long practice. Troop movements in a modern battle may be quite different to parade-ground manoeuvres but the principle is the same. Immediate response, intense comradeship and utter determination in the face of all difficulties, need to be learnt on the parade ground before they can be tested in battle.

2015 is the 200th anniversary of the Battle of Waterloo. Although a close-run thing it was ultimately won by the sort of stolid endurance, discipline and commitment shown by the British and Allied squares in the face of French artillery and cavalry attack. Their success was the fruit of parade-ground training.

This book shows in vivid illustrations every aspect of this unique ceremony. The finished product is a celebration of the Sovereign's birthday, but it is certainly not a 'theatrical' production, it is a deadly serious demonstration of the basic infantry skills for which the British Guards are renowned across the world.

Philip

The Queen's favoured piece of jewellery to be worn during her Birthday Parade is known as the Brigade of Guards brooch. It was worn by Queen Mary, whose husband, George V, created the youngest Guards regiment during the First World War. Under his imperial crown are gathered the badges of the five Foot Guards regiments.

The badge of the Grenadier Guards is at the top; beneath is the badge of the Welsh Guards flanked on the left by the Scots Guards and on the right by the Irish Guards; the Coldstream Guards badge is at the bottom. The motto, 'Quinque Juncta in Uno' ('Five Joined in One'), defines the unity of the Brigade. It was modelled on the brooch given to Queen Victoria by the officers of the Brigade in 1863.

The Queen sits on the chair designed and made for her to use at The Queen's Birthday Parade and kept at the Royal Hospital, Chelsea. She is flanked by representatives of the seven regiments of the Household Division, of which she is Colonel-in-Chief, and the King's Troop, Royal Horse Artillery, of which she is Captain General. They were assembled and photographed for this book in St George's Hall during the Windsor Court.

From left to right: WO2 (SCM) James Fitzgerald, The Life Guards; Lieutenant Kaspar Varmuza, Grenadier Guards; Captain Oli Jones, Scots Guards; Captain David Luther-Davies, Welsh Guards; Lieutenant Ollie Rostron, Irish Guards; Lieutenant Henry Dutton, Coldstream Guards; Major Robert Skeggs, King's Troop, Royal Horse Artillery; WO2 (SCM) Edward Sampson, The Blues and Royals. All except the King's Troop carry either the Sovereign's Standards or The Queen's Colours that are trooped at The Queen's Birthday Parade. The Royal Artillery have no Colours, but instead honour their guns.

THE QUEEN'S BIRTHDAY PARADE Where do you feel a nation's heartbeat? There may be any number of answers, but one can usually give the short-term visitor a reasonable suggestion with some confidence: in the United States of America it might be the Lincoln Memorial; in France, perhaps the Tomb of Napoleon; in Russia, Red Square. In all cases it is likely to be a renowned public place where people go to remember and even remake their history.

In a nation as old as the United Kingdom there are many contenders; however, one can argue that here it is not a place, but an event, that carries that heartbeat: The Queen's Birthday Parade. Yet how can an annual celebration by the five Regiments of Foot Guards, essentially a private ceremony in a public place showing, through historic military drill, their personal duty to their Sovereign and Colonel-in-Chief, stand for a whole nation?

The answer lies in the many threads of history which come together on Horse Guards Parade for the couple of hours during which the Foot Guards celebrate their Colonel-in-Chief's official birthday by trooping one of their Colours through their ranks, and parading past her with the other regiments of her Household Troops.

There may be many different views of 'Trooping the Colour': I've heard it described as 'Ruritanian flummery'; Ninette de Valois revered it as the greatest act of public choreography; to its participants, it combines sweat, discomfort, nerves and even boredom. For all of them, however, and the millions of spectators on Horse Guards and watching on television, it is a proud but affectionate compliment to the embodiment of an ideal, to our Sovereign.

The United Kingdom is not a militaristic nation. The Royal Navy and more recently the Royal Air Force have kept us free from invasion for a millennium. We only usually see our soldiers on our streets in ceremonial parades, not security operations. Our Armed Forces have always been composed of volunteer professionals; even during the two world wars, conscription was not universal; we have never adopted the idea that military service is an expression and duty of citizenship. Indeed, 10% of our Armed Forces are not British citizens at all, but come, as volunteers, from a wide range of countries. The Foot Guards regiments have many non-British personnel, not least the Irish Guards, whose many soldiers from the Republic of Ireland demonstrate the personal loyalty to the Sovereign which is such a hallmark of the Household Division.

The Queen's Birthday Parade is not only an expression of the personal loyalty of Guardsmen, but of regiments whose history is closely linked to the Sovereign. The Queen is Colonel-in-Chief of all Guards regiments; she presents them with their Standards and Colours; over the years members of the Royal Family have served

in the regiments of the Household Division, and are Colonels of most of them. The regiments guard the royal residences in London and Windsor, and play a major role in all State Ceremonial.

In every ceremony the regiments do not just do their duty, but they also represent the rest of the Armed Forces in guarding and honouring the Head of State. The meticulous preparation of uniforms, equipment and drill which make the Birthday Parade such a spectacle are not merely the self-imposed high standards of the participants; they represent the respect, affection, loyalty and pride of the whole nation.

Each uniform, Colour, manoeuvre and piece of music is redolent of our past, from the Battle Honours to the numbers of studs on the Guardsmens' boots; and like everything historic, they have current significance. The drill movements of the parade are the battle drills which won the battles of the Napoleonic Wars; it was by the disciplined perfection of their forming into line that the Foot Guards routed Napoleon's Imperial Guard at Waterloo. Drill remains at the heart of our training today: superb weapon handling and tactical movement, ingrained so deeply that they are instinctive, are still battle winners, as Major Roly Spiller's account below testifies only too clearly. Their history and modern relevance are explored in detail in this book; suffice to say here that the Birthday Parade connects the nation's past, present and future in a unique way.

"When I was leading my Troop on a long-range reconnaissance patrol in northern Helmand Province, Afghanistan, my vehicle was struck by an IED. Trooper Babakobau LG was killed instantly, and the remainder of the crew was wounded. My operator was blown clear and landed some 30 feet away, badly dazed but unhurt. I was struggling to assist the driver and interpreter, with my left arm being of little use and my left leg unable to support my weight, when I saw the operator stumbling about near where he had landed. In this potential minefield I needed to get him to stand still until the remainder of the Troop could clear a safe path to us. I shouted at him repeatedly to stay still, but he did not register and kept moving. Then I had a flash of inspiration (or desperation) – in the best parade ground voice I could muster, I shouted, 'Halt!' And he did."

Major Roly Spiller, The Blues and Royals
Adjutant of the Household Cavalry Mounted Regiment

THE HISTORY OF THE QUEEN'S BIRTHDAY PARADE The Queen is the personification of the United Kingdom and therefore the country's 'national celebration' has emerged from marking her birthday. This is a custom that the monarch's own troops, the Household Division, have helped to fashion. The tradition is now observed around the world by British embassies and high commissions; at the same time, the date has become a holiday for civil servants and is one of the two annual occasions when The Queen issues a list of those she has selected to invest with a national honour.

Birthdays have been significant milestones worthy of acknowledgement for centuries. They are one of the great human measurements of life and the template against which all age and accomplishment is measured. Much of the world itself, through the Gregorian calendar, marks its own passing years in the number that have passed since the birth of Jesus Christ. The traditions of birthday cakes and presents are locked into culture and, with the singing of 'Happy Birthday to You', translated into many of the world's languages, they grant elevation and goodwill to the day dedicated to the celebrated.

In the tradition of birthday presents, the Household Division marks its own particular loyalty and determination to protect The Queen and her nation in a precise presentation of the highest achievable standards of military excellence. This is done on behalf of all the Armed Services and the nation they defend. The reputation of the naval, air and military forces is encased in the standards each upholds and the teamwork each must instill in order to achieve success. On the parade square, exquisite rightness is an outward sign of the inherent operational effectiveness delivered, when required, in the field of humanitarian missions, peacekeeping or stark war fighting.

On the allotted 'official' birthday, now locked in to the second Saturday in June in order to avoid both interrupting the capital's traffic and also the chill spring weather of The Queen's real April birthday, more than 1,400 soldiers and officers march in precise theatre. They do this in order to mount the guard on Buckingham Palace and St James's Palace from Horse Guards Parade and do honour to The Queen's Colour, the silk flag that is carried, or 'trooped', to embody the symbolic soul of a battalion of fighting men.

Like most British ceremonial, this parade has evolved from raw military utility but over time it has gathered to itself a lexicon of acquired traditions, meaning and symbols. Nothing happens that carries no meaning. Everything has developed with purpose and its provenance is where the magic of this annual summer performance can be discovered. The unwrapping of each part of this drama exposes a clue to the needs and whims of monarchs, commanders and time. Some traditions have origins

1812
© *Bridgeman*

*The Scots Guards' Colour
leading the March Past
in slow time on the
Colonel's Review.*

2012

that are as boldly concreted into the foundations of history as is the Crown itself, while others have emerged from untraceable hearsay. But, in this narrative both weave together to deliver The Queen's Birthday Parade, or Trooping the Colour, an icon of British life that, in its exact but unlaboured drill, physically expresses something of what the United Kingdom is.

There is an ancient and military provenance to the royal livery of scarlet and gold, which is the leitmotif of the parade, expressed in the soldiers' tunics, braid and buttons. This comes from the heraldic achievement that has been borne by English Sovereigns, since the three running golden lions were first stitched onto a red field for the 'Coat of Arms' worn by the monarch for tournaments and battle over camouflaging armour by Richard I in the 12th century. Gold and scarlet also echo the colours worn by the kings of Scots from a similar period, whose rampant red lion, within a treasure flory, counter flory, combines with England's arms in the Royal Standard of today. There are glimpses of blue too, both in the sashes worn across the tunics of royal Colonels and in the uniform of The Blues and Royals and the King's Troop, Royal Horse Artillery: this draws reference to the heraldic identity of the kings of France, which consisted of golden fleurs de lys on a blue field. The French Crown was claimed by England's monarchs from the start of the Hundred Years War, by Edward III, and not fully

laid down until the 1800s, the century that saw the last challenge to French rule at Waterloo. Heraldry was the first formalised language of symbols worn by knights in battle that enabled the speedy identity of friend from foe among the chaos of combatants. Under full armour, or chain mail, a warrior was lost. But organised heraldry in both the Coats of Arms, which were worn over this body protection, carried aloft in banners and painted onto shields, preceded the development of uniforms, which themselves derived from these heraldic liveries. When The Queen arrives among her troops for her Birthday Parade and her Royal Standard is unfurled from the roof of the Horse Guards building at the strike of 11, its colours and the national identities they portray are reflected back in the uniforms gathered on the gravel below. Unmistakably, the very colours of the uniforms link her with her medieval ancestors and their war fighting.

It is a universal truth that a leader is only as strong as the force he or she leads. This military fact has been understood by monarchs, instinctively keen to hold onto power by securing their realm, since the start of time. The relationship between monarchs and those responsible for their safety was key. The way this essential trust was managed, through the vicissitudes of the national story and changing social structures, has shaped the links that now exist between The Queen and her Armed Forces in general, but with her Household Troops in particu-

lar. Each king and queen has cultivated the bonds with the men charged with guarding their body and home. With each passing year of the reign, the success of these body guards could be measured. Therefore, just as Britain has chosen to mark its passing years through the Sovereign's birthday, so it became an even more appropriate measure of the body guards' success to do the same.

The evolution of kingship itself, long before the Norman Conquest of 1066, was linked to military strength. The prerequisite for any candidate to the thrones of the ancient and pre-Christian English 'heptarchy' of seven separate kingdoms was a claim of descent from the Pagan god king Woden, deemed the exemplar of warrior leadership. His descendant candidates were tested in competition by the great men of the land, according to the mettle of their brawn and military skills. This criterion for kingship remained the most vital skill, but weight gradually swung towards wisdom and intelligence, as the role of statecraft evolved over that of basic conquest.

From the earliest recorded accounts in ancient Egypt, Greece and Rome, soldiers have been gathered in a display of power around their chief, in order to demonstrate deterrent, defend or project influence. They have been trained for battle and campaigned in expeditionary zeal. Alexander the Great reached far to the east and the Caesars into the furthest corners of the known world. With these campaigning troops often went the sym-

bols of their identity that were intended to embody the manly virtues of battle, principal of which was to elevate courage and to honour the dead. The Roman Standards were totemic icons of the legions that marched from Rome to defend the vast Empire. The significance of these objects was greater than their value because they were the soul of the force they represented and were inured with a degree of respect that matched deification. Where these objects were lodged and held in safety was of general interest to all members of the fighting force. In a precisely similar way the Colours of infantry battalions, the guns of the artillery and the Standards and Guidons of the cavalry are objects of virtual reverence to their members.

Following the Norman Conquest, England's army was based on the feudal system. Duke William of Normandy had taken possession of the kingdom root and branch. Those great Norman knights who had ventured precariously across the English Channel, in boats and barges, in order to take on and defeat the Saxon army of Harold II were rewarded with land. But this land came with strict strings attached, under a system designed to maintain royal supremacy and overlordship. Each tenant of land granted by the king held it under an agreement that he was to train and provide troops to be ready whenever the king demanded. Monarchs depended upon this state of military readiness, as did their counterparts on the Continent. Broadly, this

*Her Majesty's Body Guard
of the Honourable Corps of
Gentlemen-at-Arms in Colour
Court at St James's Palace.*

tradition of feudal armies, which were often dependent for success upon the support of the Church, developed into a standing militia.

In the Tudor period monarchs were protected by two dedicated Body Guards. It was a development in direct royal protection that followed the Wars of the Roses between the Houses of Lancaster and York. The oldest of these was the Yeomen of the Guard, established to protect Henry VII soon after his victory over the House of York in the Battle of Bosworth Field in 1485. The second was the Honourable Corps of Gentlemen at Arms, appointed by Henry VIII to be his 'closest' guard and recruited from gentlemen, or knights of the realm. Henry VII did much to heal the wounds of this period of civil war by marrying Elizabeth of York, the niece of his defeated and killed adversary, Richard III. To underscore this symbolic union between two feuding houses, Henry VII adopted a badge that combined the white rose of York with his own red Lancastrian rose. This was embroidered onto the uniforms of his Body Guards and their banners and standards displayed the same badge beneath the royal crown against the Tudor family's colours of green and silver (or white). This continued the tradition of a master using his heraldic badge to mark those in service to him, but it also marked the start of a new structure in the use of uniform and symbolism to identify royal guards.

The Tudors imbued the Crown with a new confidence in its status and power, despite the vicissitudes of religion, family differences and the ultimate lack of a direct heir. Armies were raised when required by monarchs as they saw fit and disbanded once their need was past. It was a pragmatic evolution of the feudal system. Part of this process included regular tournaments, which became great spectacles of pageantry, heraldry and ferocious danger for those tilting their powerful chargers and lances at each other. It was a sport. It was also a forum for the brave to catch the eyes of sweethearts. But, above all, it was essential training for battle. The place chosen for this activity close to Whitehall Palace was called the Tiltyard. It remains in name only as the tarmac-covered square, bounded by Horse Guards and the street called Whitehall.

When the last of the Tudors, Queen Elizabeth I, died in 1603, the galloper bearing the news to Edinburgh brought also the implicit invitation from England to the Stuart monarch James VI of Scots to head south and take possession of his cousin's fabulous Court and country. He left Holyrood under escort with indecent haste, never to return. In his mind was the very clear philosophy of how he would interpret this inheritance.

Assuming the English kingdom in addition to his Scots title, he was known as James I and VI of England, Scotland, Ireland and France. Perhaps with such titles it is unsurprising that he believed he was God's chosen, with the Divine Right to rule the newly combined kingdoms as his whim decreed. The plot on his life and his Parliament just two years later only led to further concern for his safety and protection.

This threat stemmed from the post-Reformation religious discontent that existed between the residual Roman Catholic parts of the population and the ascendant Protestants. It had been the policy of English monarchs to control Ireland for many centuries, since Henry II received the papal 'Laudabiliter' bull in 1155 giving licence for the Angevin king to impose Gregorian rules on that island. This document was cited, along with Pope Alexander III's recognition of England's kings as 'Lords of Ireland', as justification for sovereignty over the Irish. One policy used to enforce this was the deliberate imposition of Protestants onto the lands of Roman Catholics. Irish submission to the will of its neighbour was always complex. In 1641, Charles I was again minded to raise regiments to protect Scottish settlers in the north of Ireland: one raised by the Marquess of Argyll and known as his Royal Regiment, the antecedent to the regiment known today as the Scots Guards.

Charles I maintained his father's increasingly provocative view of Divine Right. It was provocative because Parliament distrusted the fact that the new king's wife was the overtly Roman Catholic Henrietta Maria, who was both a princess of France and a de Medici. Charles believed that his authority stemmed directly from God and his logic

deduced that his will was thus law and beyond question. On this issue, he fell out with Parliament, which was ironically the only unimpeachable means through which a king could levy taxation from the people in order to pay the militia and defend England. Scotland was a separate nation at this point with its own evolving military tradition. The disagreement between king and Parliament ultimately revolved around the Militia Bill, which restricted the granting of officers' commissions to Parliament, in an attempt to curb the monarch's ability to raise troops without its authority. In response to this, Charles recommended that there should be 10,000 volunteers raised to act under his sole command. Undoubtedly, troops on whom the monarch could count for loyalty, like his close guard, would be at the heart of this number. It was part of his plan to mount a coup in order to restore his position.

At this precise time, in December 1641, the king gave orders for a Court of Guards to be built in the old Tiltyard of Whitehall Palace, to ensure that the most modern facilities would house his closest protection in London. It was arguably part of the great Military Revolution, which stretched from the mid-16th to mid-17th centuries, in which armies increased in size, became of necessity more directly under central authority and were to become the stuff of statecraft. This evolution demanded more coherent organisation and this naturally implied structure, drill and formal templates for

all coherent actions. This was a language of doing business that the Foot Guards regiments would embrace and make into an art form. Secure in his defence by building the new Court of Guards, the king pounced. He marched into the House of Commons to arrest those Members averse to his will. But the plan failed. 'I see the birds have flown,' said the king, when he realised they had been warned off and escaped. The plan had backfired and it destabilised the king's position and, eventually, he fled London to be among more loyal supporters.

On 22 August 1642, in the year when the regiment that became the Scots Guards was founded, the king raised his Standard in Nottingham. There was no Royal Standard to hand and so one had to be hastily sewn together. As a symbol it was a vital emblem to represent the king's stand, but with equal symbolism in a gale that night it blew down. The king's army was eventually defeated by the better-trained and equipped New Model Army that Oliver Cromwell had established with the direction of what became known as the Long Parliament, in 1645. This army was modern and highly motivated. As the axe fell on the neck of King Charles I on 30 January 1649 it must have seemed impossible that the monarchy would ever be revived.

Charles II was living in The Hague and just 18 years old when his father was executed. Straight away, he was proclaimed king in Scotland, Jersey and in Ulster and, just as quickly, his safety was at risk

because the new king represented a rallying point for Royalists, even though the office of king was abolished within weeks. His very heartbeat was therefore a threat to the new Commonwealth. To counter this, Royalist soldiers still loyal to the cause assembled and prepared for whatever military action could possibly restore a Stuart to the throne. Among them were soldiers that would one day form the nucleus of regiments that now form part of the Household Division.

Meanwhile, Oliver Cromwell's authority increased without check. He set up the administrative headquarters for his military command of the country beside the Court of Guards, which Charles I had built at the Tiltyard. This started a tradition for the British Army (Cromwell compelled temporary unity between the nations of England and Scotland for the duration of the Commonwealth) to keep its HQ here, which lasted at Horse Guards for nearly three centuries until 1855.

Cromwell was granted almost autocratic powers, or took them through his Major Generals. Underscoring this, further regiments were raised; among them one recruited by General Monck in 1650 and called Monck's Regiment of Foot. This was the antecedent of the Coldstream Guards.

However, by Cromwell's death 1658, the British Isles were exhausted by the dismal reality of living under Puritan ideology and the endless campaigning suppression of his New Model Army.

General Monck in the Coldstream Regimental Headquarters, Wellington Barracks.

Charles II was in Holland waiting for this news but still the circumstances were hopeless for his return. The Commonwealth was to last a further two years, under Cromwell's less able son, Richard. With Richard as Lord Protector and three powerful Generals gripping power through the Army's might, the Royalist cause was weak. One of these Generals was Monck, who had been controlling Scotland since 1651.

Richard Cromwell finally resigned a hopeless position at the beginning of the summer in 1659: he had gambled away his remnant credibility by turning to the Army and against Parliament. The Commonwealth was faltering. A coup later in the year brought Monck south in response, to protect Parliament: a decision that would prove key to Charles's fortunes, though few could guess this at the time. He set off from Scotland on 1 January 1660 and reached London a month later. Still it was opaque what support he might be nurturing for the exiled monarch, but under his insistence there were free elections in April and Charles's letter to the new Speaker promising great 'esteem for Parliaments' shaped an invitation for the monarch to return after eight troubled years. Charles landed on British soil on 26 May, having been conveyed across the Channel in the ship *Naseby*, which was subtly renamed the *Royal Charles*. General Monck's reward for this was a dukedom and the award of the Order of the Garter, the star of which was to become the badge of his regiment.

The Restoration of the Crown in 1660 brought Charles II back to Britain in glory. With him came a retinue of soldiers, the Life Guards, who had kept him safe during his exile. Their reward would be seniority above all others in a new Regular Army. Much was to change after the lessons of the two civil wars, not least because, at accession, the new king had four separate armies that had to be unified into a single force.

In August the New Model Army was disbanded by Parliament and replaced by the New Standing Army, which would depend for its existence and payment on the goodwill of Parliament. There was to be no exceptions to this order but, due to a sudden threat, Monck's regiment was never properly dissolved. Instead, under his command, they laid down their weapons and picked them up again for the king.

The Coldstream Guards had, however, missed the race for precedence in the order of the new king's regiments because this place had already been granted to the men who had mustered to serve Charles in Bruges, in 1656, called simply the Royal Regiment of Foot Guards. They had provided close escorts to a grateful hunted monarch and came with the returning Sovereign to claim his throne.

Charles II and his Court faced Restoration with a pragmatic reality, huge opportunity and the advantage of goodwill. Parliament maintained its privileges but the monarch regained almost all his

George II (painted by John Wootton) at the Battle of Dettingen in 1743, the last time the monarch led the British Army in battle.
© Bridgeman

previous powers. Part of the essential royal pragmatism was recognition that Divine Right was no longer acceptable in English or Scots princes. Charles had first-hand understanding through his father's execution of the vulnerability of his office and so, professing the English Church's mantra for Faith, he held his Roman Catholic thoughts in check.

Restoration also provided the opportunity to review the military defence of the wounded realm. Families were deeply bruised by the ideological division of the previous decades and a benevolent monarch established the Royal Hospital at Chelsea to provide a home in old age for former combatants of both sides.

The loyalty of the New Standing Army was sorely tested, as was that of all who believed in Protestant government, when James II succeeded his brother in 1685. Few monarchs could have inherited such a great opportunity and been so foolish. As the son of Charles I, he might have known better than to be the overtly Roman Catholic prince he was determined to be. He inherited the New Standing Army of 20,000 men including the regiments devoted to the Sovereign's protection, and this force successfully put down the Monmouth Rebellion. However, James wanted to shape things further. He prorogued his Parliament, resolved to rule without it, and promoted Catholic officers into all the senior appointments. The nation was ever fearful of French invasion and the loss of a vulnerable Protestant status quo,

and it intervened against its king, but this time by offering the Crown, with a Bill of Rights attached, to James's daughter Mary, and his nephew William of Orange. The Glorious Revolution by which this was achieved in 1688 is so called because of the relatively low loss of life and the assured Protestant succession to the Crown that was achieved the following year.

The two new Sovereigns were immediately faced with the start of threats by James's adherents, the Jacobites, and this fear never really abated until the last of James's heirs were encased in the Vatican's

catacombs. In the opening campaign of this struggle, William III led the Army, which was supported by the English and Scots Parliaments, among which the three regiments of Foot Guards and Life Guards played their part.

The English and Scottish Armies were amalgamated with the Act of Union in 1707. They were jointly engaged along with many other allies in the War of Spanish Succession and accrued victories under the Duke of Marlborough, at Blenheim and Ramillies. There were two further great battles, at Oudenarde and Malplaquet, both of which were

claimed as victories although the latter was arguably a stalemate gained at hideous cost of life.

Queen Anne died in 1714 presenting arguably the most vulnerable moment in the natural succession. The Army was partly unsure who her heir would be. Parliament had clear intent that it would be the new Elector of Hanover, but he was in no hurry to leave the Continent for the crown awaiting him in London. Again, there was a chance that the Jacobite pretender, Anne's half-brother James Stuart, might arrive from Lorraine and fill the vacuum. In the end, James wavered and the day was lost to George I. It was known as one of the greatest missed chances of royal history. As it was, the Horse and Foot Guards had a constantly empty set of palaces to guard because of the new king's frequent absences in Hanover.

His son, The Prince of Wales, was a soldier to his bootstraps, but he was unable to retain his father's confidence, which made their relationship tortuous until George I died in 1727. During George II's reign we find the first record of orders for a ceremonial on Horse Guards Parade that sets in motion the story of Trooping the Colour. The new king celebrated his birthday on 30 October and, perhaps for this reason, a link between royal parades and this chill autumnal date was not established. He had been at the Battle of Oudenarde in 1708, fighting under the command of the Duke of Marlborough, aged 25, when

Eton schoolboys celebrating the Fourth of June, George III's birthday, on the Thames at Windsor.

the Hanoverian succession of his father was still far off. In 1743, aged 60, he was back in the saddle as king and leading his army from the front against the French at the Battle of Dettingen in the War of the Austrian Succession. He exhorted his troops, which included The Life Guards, The Blues, Grenadier, Coldstream and Scots Guards, with the encouragement, 'Now, boys, fire and behave bravely, and the French will soon run.' This active leadership worked and, perhaps inspired by their sword-wielding warrior monarch, the British Army marked with victory the last occasion when it was led in the field by a king. The battle may have been won, but the Guards were not enamoured with their monarch: they saw his extremely close links to the Hanoverian soldiery, over and above the king's own British Guards regiments, as irksome.

King George II's son, the 22-year-old Duke of Cumberland, was by his father's side on the Dettingen battlefield. Three years later he would face his cousin, the Jacobite Pretender's son, Bonnie Prince Charlie, at Drumossie Moor outside Inverness for the final battle of the 1745 rebellion. In a ruthless final fight, the victor, Cumberland, exercised merciless retribution on the defeated Highland army. The Battle of Culloden would be the last set piece battle on British soil. And no wonder; it proved to be a painful memory on the national conscience for the victors' lack of healing actions in the aftermath: a memory that has remained

and been exploited for its pain by many causes since. No Guards regiments were in the Hanoverian Order of Battle and no battle honours were awarded for the encounter. Its chief lesson to the British, who built a string of impregnable fortresses across Scotland to ensure no repeat of Jacobean revolt, was the need for fearsome organisation in the structure of the new Army. This was reflected in parades on the drill square.

Less than three years later, in 1749, the Order Books of both the Grenadier Guards and the Coldstream Guards describe the drill for trooping and lodging the Colours at the conclusion of the formal process used to change the Palace guard. The term 'Trooped the Colours' is expressed as though it was already a well-understood instruction. In detail

the writers define the number of officers, troops and musicians needed and the choreography of drill that they must collectively perform in order to honour and lodge the Colours properly. It is the first time that records define the term that would give the name 'Trooping the Colour' to subsequent parades and it underscores the respect given then, and now, to the inanimate silken symbols of a fighting force.

The last great soldier king died in 1760. Frederick, Prince of Wales, had predeceased his father and so the crown settled on George II's grandson, who became George III. Again the Household regiments adjusted their loyalties. The new king's birthday was 4 June, which would provide the catalyst for ceremony and celebration of the royal anniversary.

The date, which became a significant focus for national rejoicing as the reign lasted for 60 years, is still marked annually by Eton College in the River Thames below Windsor Castle. In 1805, just months before the Battle of Trafalgar, the king's birthday was marked at the Guard Mounting on 4 June and this traditional marking continued, albeit with occasional interruption, until 1811, when the king became ill.

There were two significant strategic military turning points in this reign. First came the loss of the American Colonies, but it was with the second great engagement, the defeat of Napoleon, that the Household Troops were fully involved in fighting for their monarch. Between these two conflagrations the British Army sank into disorganisation. It was the challenge posed by the French Revolution and all that this threatened to Britain's monarchy that galvanised into action Government and thinking strategists such as General David Dundas.

Dundas wrote a book called *Principles of Military Movements*, and its logic was closely linked to the training of troops on the parade square in order to be effective on the field of battle. It was a significant element in the rejuvenation of a military force that, in its long campaign against Napoleon, was seldom defeated.

The greatest of these battles was at Waterloo, in 1815. The precision and order of The Queen's Birthday Parade in the second decade of the 21st century echoes the squares that helped to defeat the French Imperial Army on 18 June 205 years ago. The Life Guards led the Order of Battle for the Household Brigade under Lord Edward Somerset and the 1st, 2nd (Coldstream) and 3rd Foot Guards were commanded by Generals Maitland, Cooke and Byng. The entire Anglo-Dutch Army of 68,000 troops was commanded by the future Colonel of the 1st Foot Guards, Field Marshal the Duke of Wellington.

News of the victory triggered unlimited rejoicing because it halted the further export of Napoleonic revolution across Europe. This constituted deliverance for Great Britain, at a time when its king struggled with sanity and his authority was exercised by his eldest son, George, now the Prince Regent. Despite this prince's unpopularity with Parliament for his profligacy, this victory was deemed worthy of unconfined celebration. Permission was therefore granted for the prince's extravagant plans to embellish Windsor Castle and develop Buckingham House into a palace worthy of the winning nation's Head of State. The plan would alter the Foot Guards' responsibilities. Meanwhile, the Army, while ripe for coming reform, was celebrated for its achievements and the Household Troops were increasingly identified as part of the dignifying element of the monarchy, itself the symbol of a free people now embracing the reality of worldwide Empire. This might be seen as an oxymoron today but it was understood as the opposite then.

With this national greatness came the need for show and display. The British had an abundance of symbolism and utility in the ceremonial lexicon, but the growing need for splendour would reinvent much of this into the staple of what became pageantry. This would become the outward expression that was used to display the authority of a free 'Mother country' and its royal figurehead. The British also needed splendour and form to affirm their military prowess on and across the seas and also in the politics of Europe. There was much to celebrate, and military display, with its echo of the drills that won the day at Waterloo, was the most potent catalyst. It was also a victory that brought further enduring symbolism into the traditions of the regiments of the Foot Guards. Perhaps the most visible was the adoption of the bearskin cap, worn by Napoleon's prized Imperial Guard, whose defeat broke the morale of the emperor's army at Waterloo. The 1st Guards were key in this defeat, bringing their might against the Imperial Guard's Grenadiers. They even picked up the French bearskins and replaced their own headdress. In the aftermath of Waterloo the 1st Regiment of Foot Guards was renamed the 1st or Grenadier Regiment of Foot Guards and they adopted the French grenade badge and the bearskin. The bearskin was later adopted by the other two regiments of Foot Guards, who wear it on guard outside the palaces. Thus was born the image that now shouts 'Great Britain' to

every tourist in the world.

The last three Hanoverian kings, George III, George IV and William IV, were described respectively and unkindly by Sir Sidney Lee, Victoria's first biographer, as 'an imbecile, a profligate and a buffoon'. Their reigns covered the great victory over Napoleon and its aftermath, a period of consolidation for the Army and of making do and meeting the challenges of colonial policing. Critically, the winning Army saw little need to alter its ways; after all, they had delivered success. Vested interest and the aristocratic traditions of leadership stood between the laurel wreath of Wellington's triumph and the reforms that would be vital if the Army was to be ordered properly. The Household Troops had the advantage that they were already, unquestionably, the king's own troops. But the regimental system, with its bought commissions and wealthy patronage, did little to assure a modern nation of its future security.

Royal security continued, if for no other purpose than to keep one king, George III, from view while his son ruled as Regent. The 'duties', as the detachments were called when they were dispatched to guard royal residences, variously mounted guard from their barracks or from Horse Guards Parade. The traditional attachment to Horse Guards Parade linked the mounting duties to the age-old tradition of Whitehall Palace being the residence of Tudor kingship; it also affirmed the

decision of Charles II to build his Court of Guards there. Since Henry VIII took up residence at St James's Palace, Horse Guards had been the formal entrance to the royal estate and, with the King's Life Guard as the first line of defence posted in the Tiltyard (as it still is), Horse Guards Parade was the perfect place to display to ambassadors coming to the Court at St James's, who needed to approach the king's presence through this space, that the king was well guarded, to the highest standards of discipline and drill. The Commander-in-Chief, who continued to occupy the Levee Room sited directly above the archway, could confidently look out from his vantage point, with visiting military attachés from European armies, and expect a display of the very best military traditions and skills when he surveyed the Guard Mounting. The provenance for Horse Guards Parade was impeccable and enduring. What was prone to chance was the destination of these 'duties'. They went to guard the monarch but the place of residence often changed.

The Tower of London was the first London residence of Norman monarchs, though it was deserted by kings as soon as they felt safe enough to live in a less confined way. Exceptionally, though, the guard posted there by William the Conqueror has never been relieved, making the Tower the longest-guarded building in the kingdom. It still demands the presence of the Foot Guards to protect the Regalia: the sacred symbols

A portrait of Queen Victoria, originally painted on a plaster wall, in the dining room of the Captain, Subaltern and Ensign of The Queen's Guard in St James's Palace, laid for dinner and their guests.

nessed among the iconic institutions of the nation such as its Armed Forces, had not yet taken root. In its time, therefore, the Commander-in-Chief's role as the Sovereign's representative was seen to be the most appropriate and honourable way to meet this personal salute between Household Troops and their queen.

In 1845, the aged Duke represented Victoria for the last time, as both Commander-in-Chief and Colonel of the Grenadier Guards. The crowd on Constitution Hill cheered the old hero as he rode from Apsley House to Horse Guards and the queen and her family watched from a window of Buckingham Palace. The future Edward VII was transfixed as a boy by the sight and thrilled also to see his father, Prince Albert, dressed as a Field Marshal to witness this salute to his wife. Victoria was enthralled by her hero and appointed him godfather to her third son, Arthur, named after Wellington, who went on to have a full military career and also to be Colonel of the Grenadiers.

In 1895, two years before her Diamond Jubilee, Victoria attended Guard Mounting by her Household Troops in the Upper Ward's Quadrangle at Windsor Castle. It was her 76th birthday and this was as profound a present as her own troops could offer, although they were fairly packed into the small space, with hardly room to pass a clenched fist between the arms of the parading Guardsmen. That morning, the Royal Family had accompanied Victoria in

of monarchy. After the Tower, it was Westminster Palace, which itself gave way to Whitehall and thence the Court settled at St James's Palace, where it still formally resides. The guard followed and was posted in accordance with the monarch's choice of residence. Ultimately it was posted to Buckingham House, or the Queen's House, as it was known during Queen Charlotte's reign. William IV hated the building and tried to make it the seat of Parliament after the

fire at Westminster but Queen Victoria made it her home.

Although the queen only attended her Birthday Parade once, and then not until towards the end of her reign, her interest in her Household Troops was always great, fuelled in large part by both her husband, Prince Albert, and by the Commander-in-Chief she inherited, the Duke of Wellington. Victoria and Albert were born just four years after the 'Iron Duke' had finally defeated Emperor

Napoleon at Waterloo. He was therefore the hero in both their nurseries and was lionised by a United Kingdom that owed all to the soldier deliverer. It was the tradition in the 19th century for the Commander-in-Chief to take the salute at the nominated Birthday Parade for the Sovereign. Monarchs fulfilled a distant role from public life and the influence of Prince Albert to move the Royal Family into the public arena, exercising patronage and being wit-

two carriages to watch the 1st Battalion Scots Guards troop their Colour. The grass banks below the Round Tower were scattered with people watching the parade, probably from the castle community and from the barracks in the town. Immediately in front of them, in divisions divided by the statue of Charles II, their founder, were two squadrons of The Life Guards. Over the sward of this well-kept lawn trundled the first of two open landaus with the diminutive Victoria, as ever dressed in black with a white fringed parasol, accompanied by her daughters Princess Louise, the Marchioness of Lorne and Princess Christian of Schleswig-Holstein. Returning to her apartments, the Colonel-in-Chief sent a message of satisfaction at the good drill and smart turnout of the troops. It was to be the only Birthday Parade that she attended in person, but it was repeated the very next day on Horse Guards, in order to mount the Palace Guard in proper form, with the salute taken on the queen's behalf by her first cousin, Adolphus, the Duke of Cambridge, who was Commander-in-Chief.

This Duke of Cambridge took great pleasure in this task but soon afterwards he was retired from the post. In 1870, he had already demonstrated how reluctant he was to embrace change when he refused to vacate the Commander-in-Chief's office in the Levee Room directly above the arch in Horse Guards. His civil servants had moved their headquarters to a properly constructed new location near-

ly 15 years before. Perhaps out of pity for her ageing cousin, Victoria permitted him the privilege of continuing to take the salute at future Sovereign's Birthday Parades but neglected to pass this decision on to the Chain of Command. Inevitably, chaos ensued when Lord Lansdowne, Cambridge's successor, discovered the plan. It was a slight, and in response Lansdowne refused to attend and so the queen directed that her son, The Prince of Wales, would represent her. This was one of the rare occasions when he was deployed by his mother as her direct depute in a mother–son relationship that had been strained ever since the young prince had escaped the tight

control of his Grenadier Guards governor, Major General Robert Bruce, to sleep with an actress while training with that regiment at Curragh Camp in Ireland. The ensuing parental rebuke brought the Prince Consort to his son in Cambridge during autumnal rain, only to catch the chill that triggered his fatal typhoid in 1861. Victoria would never forgive him.

For every remaining year of the ailing queen's reign, her son took the salute. It was a diplomatic solution that had the advantage of further bonding the Royal Family with, and holding anyone else from, the privilege of taking the unique salute from the Household

Troops to their Sovereign. In the last year of her reign, Victoria honoured the bravery of Irish troops fighting the Boers by creating the Irish Guards in 1900 and appointing the great hero of that battle, Lord Roberts, as their first Colonel.

Experienced at the role of attending the Guard Mounting when he acceded to the throne on 22 January 1901, Edward VII selected his mother's birth date for his first Birthday Parade as a mark of respect because his own was inconveniently in early November. The Empire was waging a deeply unpopular war in South Africa against the Boers, in which the Household Troops were heavily engaged. Considering how unpopular this war was in Europe it was all the more exceptional that Edward VII ignored Government advice and went to Paris, returning with the Entente Cordiale of 1904, which was to be the treaty by which the United Kingdom held alliance against Germany through two world wars. The Household Troops would pay heavy costs in both wars but their more senior officers remembered the solid sight of their robustly indulgent monarch packed into a bursting tunic to attend Guard Mounting, when health permitted.

His second son succeeded in 1910, as George V, and took a deep interest in his Household Troops and particularly in this parade. Conveniently his birthday fell on 3 June, the perfect date for the annual event. Following the death from influenza in 1892 of his elder brother,

Edward VII in the Mess at Knightsbridge.

ment in this national celebration one where he was more readily seen by the crowds; secondly, and more importantly, to put him directly at the head of his troops. This would underscore the reality in the mind of all troops but it would also give greater meaning to the tradition that this was the King's Birthday Parade.

Thus in 1913, on George's actual birthday, he witnessed the traditional Trooping the Colour and took the salute before taking his place at the head of the Foot Guards as they marched back down The Mall to take on their responsibilities of guarding the palaces and returning to their other duties. It brought a simple and visible reality to the parade that had not benefitted from such a symbolic logic before.

Again, it did not take the royal commander long after returning from his Birthday Parade before he was busily engaged in making further tweaks. The Major General received more letters with good ideas from the Private Secretaries, which clearly contained points that came directly from the king himself. These improved still further the idea that this parade was a personal matter between the Sovereign and his own troops. It also must have been affirming for London District to have this level of personal interest from an active and engaged figurehead. The carefully wrought plans limited the number of mounted officers who would ride with the king in order not to dilute the visual effect of this Dettingen-style royal leadership, from

Prince Albert Victor, George became his father's heir at the age of 26. Immediately, his naval eye for detail and punctiliousness were applied to everything and he particularly relished ceremonial form and order.

The new king emperor attended his first Guard Mounting at Horse Guards in 1912 and it would prove to be the catalyst for improvements that would shape it as a more logical event that more closely and visibly bonded him with his troops.

In the remaining years of peace, the king, with his energetic military Private Secretary, Sir Fritz Ponsonby, would develop with the help of the Major General Commanding London District a structured narrative for the Sovereign's involvement as Colonel-in-Chief, from which there has since been virtually no change. The parade had not been held in the two previous years because of Court Mourning for his father in 1910 and the extensive preparations for his coronation

in 1911. When the first Trooping the Colour of George V's reign was held it was spectacularly well executed. It came soon after the nation had witnessed their new king make an impressive imperial visit to India, firmly establishing him as an active and increasingly constitutional figurehead for the Empire.

Not long after the 1912 parade, the king was already thinking how better to shape the ceremony in order to deliver two outputs: first, to make his involve-

the front. Indeed, in order to make the effect more profound, the king directed that the Household Cavalry's preceding escort should leave a clear 100 yards between their rear and the nose of the king's horse, because some bunching up had occurred the year before.

The scarlet-clad display of perfect drill that took place on Horse Guards towards the end of June 1914 was the culmination of the troops' hard work to bring the king's plan to reality. At the end, the contented Sovereign led his troops back to Buckingham Palace, accompanied by just the mounted members of the Royal Family and the Field Officer in Brigade Waiting, who had commanded the parade, with the Major General and an equerry in attendance. They followed the Household Cavalry and the Massed Bands of the four Guards regiments. In front of the Centre Gate, the king took the salute of the Horse and Foot Guards as they returned to their barracks, while the King's Guard marched into the Palace with the freshly trooped Colour. Then, just as he had personally envisaged, the king turned about and rode into the Palace through the old and new guards before the Changing of the Guard was completed, which had always been the reason for this ceremonial. It locked the Sovereign into the heart of his Birthday Parade and he was seen to be both the troops' commander and the one they existed to guard. The Queen still follows her grandfather's template and the crowds along The Mall probably

George V wearing the uniform of The Royal Dragoons in the Mess at Knightsbridge.

assume the symbol of her lone leadership of the parade is centuries old rather than just over 100 years.

Within a month of the 1914 parade ground falling quiet again, the peace of Europe, which was still mostly ruled by crowned heads, many of whom were the king's relations, was shot away with a royal assassination in Sarajevo. Before the King's Birthday Parade was held again, nine million people would be dead, including many of the soldiers who had followed their king down The Mall. The Great War would even threaten the stability of George V's reign.

In response to the mobilisation, the Horse Guards and Foot Guards put away their Home Service Clothing (the ceremonial uniforms of the Household Division), and stored their bearskin caps in metal tins to dissuade moths. The presumption was that the fighting would be concluded before Christmas. While Headquarters London District planned military training for operations, some of the staff presumed upon a parade to mark the king's birthday on 3 June 1915. However, instead of delivering the pageantry that celebrates a nation at peace, the troops would be dug into trenches preparing for the Battle of Loos. It would be six long years before tunics would parade on Horse Guards again to mount the King's Guard.

What did happen in 1915 was the creation of a new regiment, the Welsh Guards. Within weeks of their establishment, the regiment's special bond to the Crown was confirmed by mounting the King's Guard on 1 March, the day of Wales's patron saint David. There could be no more appropriate or symbolic inauguration for the fifth regiment of Foot Guards, and months later they were in the trenches.

The Prince of Wales followed most young men of his age and joined up. In his case, it was the Grenadier Guards, though he railed against the restrictions placed upon him, as anyone might when set aside as special among a military fighting force. But he joined his father

*Edward, Prince of Wales,
the 1st Colonel of the
Welsh Guards, in the
Garrison Sergeant Major's
office in Horse Guards.*

on the morale-raising visits the king emperor made to the Western Front and they seldom failed to visit the Household Troops.

It took several months following the Armistice in 1918 to get the Guards Division safely back to London's barracks. No one believed hostilities could return but, arguably, it was an armistice and not surrender, until the terms of the Treaty of Versailles both closed off the Great War and signalled the countdown to 1939. The aristocratic families that had provided sons to the officer corps of the Household Troops had borne a higher burden of casualties than almost any other section of British society, such was the fatal nature of leadership in trench warfare.

Lloyd George promised the returning combatants that he would create a nation fit for heroes. It was into this returning normality that plans to mark the king's birthday were hatched and, on 3 June, the biggest Guard Mounting ever staged, before or since, was held in Hyde Park. It was not possible to gather in Horse Guards Parade because the temporary structures built there to provide wartime administrative space had not yet been removed. Tunics and bearskins, put away in 1914, were still mothballed and so the troops paraded in the khaki battle dress they had fought in. The 3rd Battalion Coldstream Guards mounted the guard on the Palace from this grassy parade ground and therefore trooped their King's Colour.

On that day the king appointed The Prince of Wales, who had ridden beside his father as a boyish-looking Grenadier, as Colonel of the Welsh Guards. It was a further step in the re-creation of a recognised separate identity for the Principality of Wales within the United Kingdom, something Lloyd George was determined to develop as a by-product of his premiership.

The king further bonded his family into the parade by having his sons in the procession, when possible. Prince Albert, the Duke of York, started attending in the uniform of the newly established Royal Air Force but, in 1933, he was appointed Colonel of the Scots Guards. The prince joined his elder brother and his great-uncle, the Duke of Connaught, Colonel of the Grenadiers, in Tunic Order. Among the many accoutrements the Duke of York was supplied with was a Levee Sword of his new regiment, which became and is still a significant instrument of the monarchy. Wherever his daughter, Queen Elizabeth II, travels today this sword goes too because it is the instrument she has chosen to deliver the accolade of knighthood to any of her subjects selected to receive this honour. Oddly, considering that Full Dress Ceremonial uniform was worn by the princes, the king had dictated that Broad Ribbands of the Order of the Garter would not. Had it been one of the Collar Days, which are mostly religious festivals, when the Collars (or shoulder chains) are worn, then each would still have worn the sash of their second order. It is possible that his decision was to leave the grouping of tunic buttons clear for the better identification by the soldiers of their regimental Colonels.

George V's personal interest in developing Guard Mounting from Horse Guards and Trooping the Colour into the unmistakable spectacle and template of a King's Birthday Parade endures: it visibly bonds the Household Troops in a very personal salute to and led by their commanding Sovereign. Any sadness felt when he so publicly slipped from life in 1936 was assuaged by the people's enthusiasm for the vivacious heir, who chose his grandfather's name to reign as Edward VIII.

In the moment of accession he assumed the appointment as Colonel-in-Chief of all the Household regiments and they all paraded in the State Funeral. One senior Sergeant acted particularly swiftly when he stooped, over two steps no doubt, to pick up the diamond cross that had come loose and fallen from the Imperial State Crown that sat on the king's coffin. It landed in the street gutter. It contained the sapphire that had reputedly been taken from the finger of Edward the Confessor by Henry III when the Saxon saint's tomb was opened, and which legend associated with St John the Evangelist. It was a profound symbol of English kingship.

As the spectators gathered in the stands for the first King's Birthday Parade of the new reign, on 23 June 1936, few could have been aware of the significance of Mrs Ernest Simpson taking her seat. Nor could any have guessed at the anxiety in the heart of another spectator, sitting relatively close by. The Prime Minister, Stanley Baldwin, knew the political reality of the king's gathering

George VI takes the salute in 1947. Princess Elizabeth rode as Colonel, Grenadier Guards, in a uniform designed by her father.
© AP/PA

George VI as Colonel-in-Chief, Royal Horse Guards (The Blues).

intent to marry this woman, the wife of a cuckolded former Coldstream Guards officer. Quite apart from planning to challenge the social and moral attitudes of the entire Empire in this more judgemental time, King Edward was taking his salute from the Household Troops while living in breach of the strict code of conduct expected of all his Guards officers. The Royal Household had fulfilled the king's wishes by obtaining a ticket in the stand for her and perhaps had persuaded him not to put her in the Levee Room itself, where Queens Mary and Alexandra had watched their husbands take the salute.

The king had been a superlative Colonel of the Welsh Guards, getting to know most of the Sergeants' Mess well by deploying his effortless charm. The Guards were as delighted as the nation was that this debonair new monarch was the king emperor because the far-flung lands were still recovering from the horror of war. After all, he represented the lost generation and he had made many visits in recent years to France to attend the unveiling of countless British and colonial war memorials. He had served in the Grenadier Guards during the great struggle and, not knowing what was in his heart, the British could not believe their luck with this superstar.

His Birthday Parade came during the Court's mourning period for his father, so the left arms of the officers were adorned with black armbands. There were some small changes because the new king liked change; he felt the need of it in everything, as though desperate to reinvent the institution of monarchy itself. Had his reign extended, it might be fair to assume his reforms would have reached into the soul of Horse Guards itself. The riding boots were done away with for mounted Guards officers and 'overalls' took their place. Edward had always fought his father and wore trousers pressed, like overalls are, 'fore and aft', to deliberately annoy. George V considered anyone who did not wear trousers pressed from side to side caddish. The change that must have relieved the troops most was not the king's. It was the replacement of the greatcoat with a cape, which was to be worn on the back webbing in such a way that, when precisely folded, the top would be in line with the piping on the back of the collar.

Whatever hopes the Empire may have had for their new king emperor they were dashed when he clashed with his Government over his determination to marry Mrs Simpson. High standards were expected of a king, especially so after his generation had made such sacrifices for the idea of the Crown in war. For the Guards regiments, it was particularly uncomfortable because the idea of abdication made the institution of monarchy, to which they were sworn especially to serve, seem newly vulnerable. It was an entirely un-British concept and so the burden of holding the institution intact fell to the far less effervescent Prince Albert.

The new king's first decision was a wise one. He chose to reign in the same name used by his father and became King George VI. This provided reassuring continuity in the institution and connected a man whom many thought might not be up to the task, owing to his difficulty speaking in public, with George V's proven brand.

At this time, the BBC was developing the new medium of television and was pioneering outside broadcasting, in effect coverage of just about anything that moved in order to have product for transmission at a moderate cost. Trooping the Colour was a perfect candidate because it was a significant national event that had the Sovereign in view. BBC managers persuaded the relatively conservative Royal Household and London District that televising the parade would be a good idea and, therefore, in 1938 it was filmed for the first time. The power of this medium was to bring a totally new discipline to the military world and exact a demanding perfection from its participants as every error would show. Permission to film was restricted to one year but the practice has become intrinsic to the event itself and, through it, British pageantry has gained a worldwide reputation for stylish, purposeful and unprovocative display. The Guardsmen have also acquired an iconic profile that identifies the nation. Again, war clouds loomed and the sky above London swarmed with the threatening fury of Hitler's Luftwaffe. The city and nation

Cecil Beaton's portrait taken in 1942. This picture has always been in the Regimental Quartermaster of the Grenadier Guards' office in Wellington Barracks.

were connected, as never before, with the reality of a vital military struggle in which the king's Household Troops were fully committed. Battle Honours from D-Day to Berlin are embroidered across all the Regimental Colours that are trooped today.

In the very moment that George VI breathed his last at Sandringham on 6 February 1952, the Guardsmen of his King's Company of the Grenadier Guards faced their final service. In the following days, they prepared to place their shoulders under the coffin of this final British emperor, who had been called to sovereignty without preparation but who had proved a rock-like figurehead in war and played his part, as they had, to deliver a thankful victory. This was in the minds of all who watched the obsequies unfold. The King's Company's especial service is redolent of the extraordinary relationship that thrives between soldiers and their monarch. In the same moment of his death, the company changed its name from King's to Queen's Company; the last time this had happened was in 1837, 115 years before. They were joined in this doleful salute by all the regiments of the Household Division, made up of soldiers who were also preparing to change their badges and buttons from the livery symbols of a king to that of a new queen. A second Elizabethan age dawned and the new Colonel-in-Chief of the Household Division was just 25. One month after the funeral, the rehearsals would begin

for the first Trooping of the new reign and, for the first time in the memories of most, there would be a Queen's Birthday Parade.

The new Queen first commanded her own troops at the Birthday Parade on 5 June 1952 but she had been the focus of this great national pageant before. She had taken her father's place at the last King's Birthday Parade of his reign. On Thursday 7 June 1951, she had ridden side-saddle, as Colonel of the Grenadier Guards, to watch her 3rd Battalion troop its Colour while George VI rested on doctor's orders. Her father had designed the scarlet Grenadier tunic that she wore for the first time. He also supervised the tricorn cap that Danish milliner Aage Thaarup shaped from bearskin. After the parade, she wrote to the Major General explaining how proud she was to 'take the parade for the first time'. A year later, so much had changed for the Princess. Her relatively simple life as the wife of a young naval commander, spent in stations such as Malta, was over and the burden of sovereignty made her the object of the nation's self-celebration.

Just five months into her reign, on the first Thursday in June 1952, she rode out from the Centre Gate of Buckingham Palace on a chestnut horse called Winston, the name of her proud and watching war-winning Prime Minister. Once again, she was a monarch who had to hold an 'Official Birthday', as her own falls on 21 April. Her mother, the widow Queen Elizabeth the Queen

Mother, travelled by carriage to Horse Guards minutes ahead, dressed in black, smiling and waving through her grief, accompanied by Princess Margaret.

Lieutenant Colonel Angus Cameron of the 2nd Battalion Scots Guards was the Field Officer in Brigade Waiting and in command of the parade, his Military Cross a reminder of the recent war. Perhaps as a portent of the cuts that this reign would see across the Armed Forces, there were just five Guards marshalled on the parade ground instead of the traditional eight. It was also to be a second chance for Regimental Sergeant Major Fraser, who had been stood by as Sergeant Major of Escort at the Birthday Parade in 1948, which had been cancelled because of bad weather. The Queen reached Horse Guards arch, looked up to her mother standing by the Levee Room window, and saluted. Turning, she received the first royal salute of what was now her Household Division. Accompanied by her uncle, the Duke of Gloucester, she inspected the Guards and, following her express wish, the Pipers were marched to the front of the Massed Bands in order to accompany the Quick March of the Scots Guards as they gave their salute in quick time: a tradition that has continued.

The following year was dominated by the coronation on 2 June. The Household Division played its full part in that ancient ceremonial wrapped in symbolism when skies that were planned to be clear were filled with torrential rain. Everyone was completely soaked and so all

the State and Home Service Clothing had to be dried out. The white Blanco that is applied carefully to buff belts had run into the scarlet cloth and had to be brushed out. Ammunition boots were stuffed with coronation newspapers in order to dry them thoroughly enough to take fresh bulling with black polish, and Brasso had to be applied to tarnished buttons. All had to be ready for The Queen's Birthday Parade on 11 June. The Queen was accompanied by The Duke of Edinburgh for the first time, dressed as a Field Marshal, which proved a boon when his horse played up. He overcame its obstinacy with a sharp prod from the highly decorated gilt baton of his rank. Although the baton was bent by this exigency the parade went well.

The Queen chose to identify directly with her Household Division troops from the outset. Her decision to wear the scarlet tunic each year echoed her forebears. In the ensuing years, she donned the uniform of each regiment as Colonel-in-Chief, with her appearance in the Welsh Guards tunic in 1965. The Second World War had galvanised women into the Armed Services and seeing them in uniform was commonplace from 1939. This reign would see the role of women in the Armed Forces change exponentially. It was not many years before that, as Heir Presumptive, Princess Elizabeth had served as a lorry-driving subaltern in the Auxiliary Territorial Service. She had worn uniform then, and as Colonel, Grenadier Guards, but,

Princess Elizabeth taking the salute as Colonel, Grenadier Guards, in 1952.

on her accession, her decision always to wear the uniform of her Guardsmen designed by her father, and worn by her father, uncle, grandfather and great-grandfather was potent. The result became iconic of the successor to that other Elizabeth, who had inspired the loyalty of troops facing the Armada.

In 1959, the parade was held on a Saturday. The decision to move it to the weekend lifted from London an enormous burden for traffic. The quantity of cars, buses and lorries was not as great as it is now. Nor was there the added reality of threat and terrorism, which creates its own pressures on freedom and events. The result of the Saturday decision was therefore one of great foresight.

It is seldom that in the life of a queen regnant there should be the death of a king but this happened in 1972. On 28 May news came that The Queen's uncle, the former King Edward VIII, had died in Paris. It is impossible to know the real emotion that his reigning niece must have felt but her commitment was clear: there should be some gesture for the Duke of Windsor at Trooping the Colour on 3 June, less than a week later. The Act of Remembrance was powerful. The Queen reached her saluting base and a roll of drums began a minute's silence. Many watching may have tried to imagine the thoughts of Queen Elizabeth the Queen Mother, who was wearing Court Mourning in the Levee Room above. The Queen wore a black armband around her Coldstream Guards

H.M. THE QUEEN. **TROOPING THE COLOUR** A TUCK CARD
WHEN H.R.H. THE PRINCESS ELIZABETH TAKING THE SALUTE

tunic, as did all the officers. A further roll of drums ended the silence before the Pipers played a lament for the king, who had been a piper himself. After this The Queen's Birthday Parade began.

In 1981, the core role of the Household Division was profoundly tested. In the context of the force evolving from history, as a Body Guard to the monarch, the Birthday Parade was formed up and awaiting The Queen's arrival, when Marcus Sarjeant fired six blank shots at her from a starting revolver. Adept in the saddle, she was shaken but unharmed, though the horse did react. One of the street liners from the 2nd Battalion Scots Guards, Lance Corporal Galloway, leapt from the 'Present Arms' to grab Sarjeant and brought him down before police arrived. This act of instinctive courage underscored the purpose of the parade, but the action of Lance Corporal Galloway was never properly marked by the nation. The parade proceeded as planned and most spectators only discovered what had happened after The Queen had played her part and led her troops home.

The next year, on the very anniversary of this attack, 13 June, Lance Corporal Galloway was among the soldiers fighting for the liberation of the Falkland Islands. The Queen's Birthday Parade had fallen the day before. Out of respect for The Blues and Royals, Scots and Welsh Guards taking part in the military action, Major General Desmond Langley recommended a silence be kept. The Queen agreed and, during its quiet, straight after the first royal salute and after the parading Guardsmen had ordered their arms, the link between the role of ceremonial excellence and combat capability was profoundly defined, because most knew that the Welsh Guards had suffered terrible losses on board the RFA *Sir Galahad* three days before. At the end of the parade, The Queen led her troops to their duties to the strains of 'Heilan' Laddie' and 'The Rising of the Lark', quick marches that represented Scots and Welsh Guards. The procession marched through South Atlantic weather on The Mall when a massive downpour soaked monarch and men alike.

The Queen's reign has often seen Trooping the Colour coincide with the operational engagement of her Household Troops. The longest lasting such engagement was in Northern Ireland, where both a complicated history and the unique position of the Irish Guards made the domestic discomfort for this celebration of the kingdom more poignant. But there was also the advance to Pristina airport, in Kosovo, which took place on 12 June 1999, the same day as the parade. The engagements in Iraq and Afghanistan have focused the nation's awareness of the Armed Forces' commitment and sacrifice. The Birthday Parade has provided a microscope on the links between the men fighting from Forward Operational Bases through television and those, either recently returned or soon to deploy, marching

The Queen leading the Inspection as Colonel-in-Chief, Coldstream Guards, on Burmese, in 1985, followed by the Royal Colonels, including, to her immediate left, Jean, Grand Duke of Luxembourg, Colonel, Irish Guards.

round Horse Guards Parade before the Colonel-in-Chief.

The horse Burmese was retired from service as The Queen's mount after the 1986 Birthday Parade. She lived a further four years but the monarch decided not to replace her. 1986 was also the year when The Queen marked her own 60th birthday. Thus, in 1987 she left Buckingham Palace in the Ivory Mounted Phaeton, a small carriage favoured by Queen Victoria because it provided a clear view. The Queen also set aside the five regimental uniforms that she had worn year by year in favour of a dress with one feature, the brooch with badges of the five Guards regiments that her grandmother, Queen Mary, had worn.

Also in 1987 the special honour of wearing a gold set of aiguillettes, complete with the monarch's cypher, or initials, on its two points, was granted to the Major General Commanding the Household Division for commanding 'the Sovereign's personal guards'. Aiguillettes represent the ropes once carried by those in attendance to tether the principal's horse when he or she dismounted. The honour was a further demonstration of the special relationship that has continually developed in this reign between monarch and personal troops. It was once so respected that senior officers removed the aiguillettes when they demitted office but this respect has now slipped and many are worn today under less clear rules. This privilege is still maintained and properly

The Queen as Colonel-in-Chief, Scots Guards, the last time she rode in the parade in 1986. She is wearing her tunic with medals including those she earned in the Second World War.

respected by the Major General, and the Field Officer in Brigade Waiting who was granted The Queen's aiguillettes in 1990.

This is still a parade where the narrative is enhanced by the smallest details as it is this that motivates the soldiers by keeping their attention on the same minute detail. The broadcast commentaries of Trooping the Colour have often focused on the number of buttons here, or the provenance of a sword there. And, as the power to interrogate the preparations for this ceremony has increased, so the regiments have delivered story after story with endless angles on the multifarious details that go into the preparations, both for the individual soldier and from the Major General's discussions with The Queen and The Duke of Edinburgh on macro plans for change.

To mark The Queen's 80th birthday in 2006 and at her Diamond Jubilee, new precedents were set. Unlike previous Sovereigns who ruled this long, she is the first to be involved in the active exchange of loyalties with the Household Division. On both occasions, The Queen's Birthday Parade concluded in accordance with its purpose and provenance, by delivering the New Guard to the forecourt of Buckingham Palace, in order to take over as the new Queen's Guard. But on these two occasions, they then formed up underneath the great balcony from which Victoria once witnessed the salute of troops returning from the Crimean War. Reviving a

tradition of the 18th and 19th centuries, and using blank ammunition, they fired a salute, known as a Fire of Joy, or *Feu de Joie*. Just as The Queen's foot tapping during the troop by Massed Bands gives observers pleasure, so the inevitable reaction to a spray of rifle fire in such a confined area gives witnesses a similar moment of humour.

Cuts reduced the number of Guards from eight to six in the 'L' shaped formation on Horse Guards Parade in 1993, while the 2nd Battalions of the Grenadiers, Coldstream and Scots Guards were placed in suspended animation. However, the identity and the Colours survived. Hence, in what are now termed the Public Duties Incremental Companies, all the 2nd Battalion traditions are maintained. The 2nd Grenadiers are called Nijmegen Company, the 2nd Coldstream are Number 7 Company, and F Company is the name held by the 2nd Scots Guards.

One of the greatest inclusions has been the parading of the King's Troop, Royal Horse Artillery. At every Queen's Birthday Parade, the King's Troop fired The Queen's Official Birthday Gun Salute in Green Park at 11:00 but were held from the parade itself, as it was not part of the Household Division. In 1998 it was proposed that it should parade with its guns as part of the Household Division and take part in the Trooping the Colour parade. Because the teams of horses pull their 13-pounder guns, which symbolically act as Colours, the precedent

The Queen arriving for her Birthday Parade, accompanied by The Duke of Edinburgh, Colonel of the Grenadier Guards and Senior Colonel of the Household Division, in the Ivory Mounted Phaeton built for William IV.

that this gives the Royal Horse Artillery prominence over all other regiments is respected and they pass by The Queen first in the mounted walk and trot past.

One of the great sadnesses for the parade, as cuts have stripped the Armed Forces, has been the reduction in the number of musicians in the Massed Bands of the Household Division. The Guards bands that once fielded 360 musicians now field just 200, in ten ranks of 20. This has meant a gradual evolution to the impossibly complicated spin wheel.

Her Majesty's 68-year relationship with the Household Division as the Colonel-in-Chief of its seven regiments and Captain General of the Royal Artillery's members of the division, formed by the King's Troop, Royal Horse Artillery, has evolved viscerally. It stems from her own wartime experience when much of her family's close security was in the hands of these regiments. Her eye for the detail laid before her annually is guided by this longevity and her equine expertise. She has a knack for spotting the very same tiny error that the Brigade Major might and this only helps to keep standards meaningful to those determined to demonstrate their best. Just as she watched the good and bad news brought to her father in the war, so she has been the first to hear bad news and carry the burden of Armed Service personnel killed on active duty in her name.

Gradually, like George V, she has gathered around her from her own family Colonels for the Household Division regiments. Traditionally, this is never extended to the Coldstream Guards but now she has her husband, eldest son, daughter, grandson and first cousin as Colonels of the Grenadiers, Welsh, Blues and Royals, Irish and Scots Guards. The Duke of Cambridge is the first member of the Royal Family to hold the Colonelcy of the Irish Guards.

In 2015, just days before the nation marked the 200th anniversary of the defeat of Napoleon at Waterloo, which was the greatest deliverance Britain has achieved after the defeat of Hitler and fascism, The Queen arrived at precisely 11:00 in front of Horse Guards to receive the salute of the Household Division. She inspected her troops, witnessed Trooping the Colour and then led them to their Guard Changing duties. After the King's Troop guns had fired their salute and the Royal Air Force flown its saluting flypast back to stations, after Her Majesty had vacated the balcony and the majority of soldiers had dispersed to barracks there remained, on duty and ever watchful, The Queen's Guard and The Queen's Life Guard. This collective guard carries forward a baton on the monarch's defence that links them directly with the first piquet posted by the victorious conqueror William, in 1066.

For The Queen – and her descendants no doubt – this simple tradition of mounting guard will continue to give the United Kingdom an opportunity for national celebration. It is, after all, the Nation's Day.

A Captain of The Life Guards in Gold Kit, Mounted Review Order.

THE LIFE GUARDS The most senior regiment in the British Army, with their distinctive red tunics and helmets with white plumes, The Life Guards were originally three separate troops of Horse Guards. The first was formed from the gentlemen who went into exile with Charles II after the Battle of Worcester, and who guarded him in France and Holland in the 1650s. The second was formed from the gentlemen who guarded the Duke of York, the king's brother and heir to the throne, and who returned with him to England in 1660, while the third had rather different origins, having originally been Cromwell's Lord Protector's bodyguard who now protected General Monck.

After the Restoration the troops continued to attract 'private gentlemen', and competition for places, which carried the high daily rate of 4 shillings, was fierce. Their duties were onerous, with significant threats against both the king and his brother, and from the time of the Popish Plot the offices of Silver Stick and Gold Stick were introduced whereby the Colonels of the Troops of Horse Guards undertook responsibility for the Sovereign's personal safety. After Monck's death his troop became The Queen's Troop, and later a fourth Scottish Troop was added which lasted until the Union.

In the 1680s the Horse Guards were augmented with troops of Horse Grenadier Guards, who were intended to carry grenades after the French fashion but it proved one of Charles II's less successful experiments and soon the Horse Grenadier Guards became another element in the king's military household, performing royal security duties alongside the Horse Guards. They saw action in the Jacobite Wars in Flanders and Ireland, including the Battle of the Boyne in 1690. In the War of the Austrian Succession the regiment's first Battle Honour was won, at the Battle of Dettingen in 1743.

Throughout the 18th century they faced a dilemma: were they part of the deployable army or was their priority to stay in London to protect the monarch? Duties in London included not only escorting the Royal Family and taking part in major ceremonial, but also finding the daily King's Life Guard at Horse Guards, a duty continued by the Household Cavalry to this day.

The Life Guards' duties also frequently involved policing duties and crowd control, something the soldiers did not particularly enjoy. It was not until the 1780s, when the Horse Guards and Horse Grenadiers were formed into two regiments of Life Guards, taking their place in the regular army, that this conflict started to be resolved. The old concept of 'private gentlemen' was replaced with soldiers directly recruited and non-commissioned officer ranks were introduced for the first time. From 1788 The Life Guards became some of the Army's more innovative regiments, instituting a new method of riding school for training soldiers and starting to send officers to the recently founded Staff College.

Lieutenant General Sir Edward Smyth-Osbourne, Gold Stick-in-Waiting and Colonel of The Life Guards. The Gold Stick lies next to his helmet. It has the royal seal on the top mounted so that it can be seen through the peephole of a closed door. The appointment of Gold Stick-in-Waiting is shared between the Colonels of the British Army's two most senior regiments that make up the Household Cavalry, The Life Guards and The Blues and Royals. The post was created by Charles II at the time of the Popish Plot, out of fear for his life. The office holder would be directly responsible for the Sovereign's safety, in constant attendance 'from his rising to his going to bed… carrying in his hand an ebony staff or truncheon with a gold head engraved with His Majesty's cipher and crown.' Today the duties are largely ceremonial, accompanying the Sovereign when riding, travelling by carriage or walking through London. Behind the Colonel is Sir Alfred Munnings's portrait of The Life Guards drum horse Paddy II, who is 'standing out' to take the weight of the drums. Photographed in the Officer's Mess Knightsbridge Barracks

The Life Guards deployed to the Peninsula and later fought with particular distinction at Waterloo. The 2nd Life Guards took the greatest percentage of casualties of any British regiment engaged that day, taking part in the Household Brigade charge against D'Erlon's Corps and then making repeated charges against Marshal Ney's cavalry as the afternoon wore on, during which their commanding officer, Samuel Ferrior, was mortally wounded after making 11 charges. Corporal John Shaw, the famous bare knuckle fighter who was on the point of challenging for the all-England championship, was also killed, being found surrounded by the bodies of dead Frenchmen. Captain Kelly, after killing a French Cuirassier officer, calmly dismounted during the battle and cut off the epaulettes as a trophy.

Suffering from the military inactivity that afflicted the Victorian army, The Life Guards argued hard to be included in the expedition to Egypt in 1882, where they took part in the famous moonlit charge at Kassassin, and to Sudan in 1884, where they fought on camels in the expedition to relieve Khartoum. Subsequently they served alongside The Blues in a composite regiment in the Boer War from 1899 to 1900. Only one horse that had sailed out to Africa with them returned, Freddy, who had joined the 2nd Life Guards as a four year old in 1897. He took part in every action in which the regiment was engaged, covered 1,780 miles, always ridden by Corporal of Horse Stephens,

and only had 48 days off. After the war he led the regimental Musical Ride, proudly wearing his campaign medals, and when he died in 1911 he was buried under the regimental parade ground in Windsor.

After the Boer War the Household Cavalry succeeded in having one of their three regiments permanently in the Army's deployable corps, and in 1914 a composite regiment of Life Guards and Blues duly deployed to Belgium. They took part in the retreat from Mons and found themselves defending the Ypres salient in late October 1914 as the Germans made their bid to cut off the Channel Ports. The subsequent action at Zanvoorde was to be the second blackest day in The Life Guard's history, with nearly half their number in the Composite Regiment killed on Zanvoorde Ridge when intense German pressure finally forced them to retreat.

Finding little use for their horses thereafter, both 1st and 2nd Life Guards became Machine Gun troops, a role which the soldiers found more fulfilling than awaiting a breakthrough for the cavalry to exploit but which never came. In the post-war Army reductions 1st and 2nd Life Guards amalgamated to form The Life Guards.

In the Second World War The Life Guards again formed two composite regiments with The Blues. 1st Household Cavalry Regiment deployed to Palestine on horses initially and then fought through North Africa and Italy

with the 8th Army on armoured cars, while 2nd Household Cavalry Regiment crossed the Channel soon after D-Day and fought as armoured reconnaissance soldiers through France and Germany. After 1945 they served partly in Germany, sometimes on armoured cars, and partly on tanks, a squadron of which was deployed to the Gulf in 1991. Alternating with The Blues in Windsor, they also sent troops around the globe as Britain negotiated its sometimes complex drawdown from empire. Later deployments included Cyprus, in support of UN forces, and Northern Ireland.

In the post-Cold War Army reductions The Life Guards formed a union with The Blues and Royals, with two thirds of the regiment serving as formation reconnaissance in Windsor and one third as The Life Guards Mounted Squadron with the Household Cavalry Mounted Regiment in London. Since the union took place the regiment has been as busy as ever, with almost continuous deployments to Bosnia and Kosovo, then to Iraq and subsequently Afghanistan. 2015 was the first year the Household Cavalry had not been planning for a deployment since 1989, but who knows what uncertainties the world now holds. The senior regiment in the British Army, and the Sovereign's personal guard, will be ready to uphold at all times their motto, 'Honi soit qui mal y pense' – 'Evil be to him who evil thinks'.

In the highly distinctive uniform of white plumed helmet, silver cuirasse,

red tunic, gauntlets and jackboots, a Life Guard is a fine sight. Indeed, of all Charles II's standing army, his personal Life Guard was, even then, the most gorgeously attired. Count Cosmo III of Tuscany, in his *Travels Through England 1669*, described the King's Own Troop as wearing red breeches and stockings, with red jackets richly ornamented with gold lace on a royal blue background and white feathers in their broad brimmed hats. The uniform that now impresses worldwide audiences when on display in Public Duties and State Ceremonial began to emerge in the late 18th century. Perhaps its most recent quirk is the 'onion', the carefully shaped ball at the top of the white plume on the helmet. This began when the regiment had to relearn ceremonial duties after the Second World War. Corporate memory had been lost to the war, and soldiers began to carry their helmets by looping a forefinger around the top of the plume, creating a ring around the top. This was deemed smart and was made uniform – a habit resisted, however, by The Blues and Royals.

In turn with its red-plumed colleagues, The Life Guards form the daily Queen's Life Guard at Horse Guards Parade. When Her Majesty is in London, a Long Guard is mounted consisting of a 15-strong column, which leaves Hyde Park Barracks at 10:28 on weekdays (an hour earlier on Sundays). It is led by a trumpeter on a grey horse, in contrast to the cavalry blacks, while an officer

Led by Major General Sir Simon Cooper, The Life Guards' old comrades march to the Cavalry Memorial in Hyde Park to take part in the Combined Cavalry Old Comrades Association Annual Parade and Service. They are dressed in the traditional plain clothes worn in London of hard felt (or coke) hats and stiff collars, and carrying tightly furled regulation size umbrellas. Umbrellas are only to be unfurled if there is a woman in distress. The Cavalry Memorial represents St George on horseback stepping over a defeated dragon, with a frieze of galloping horsemen around the base. It originally commemorated members of the Cavalry Regiments killed during the First World War and contains bronze from guns captured during the conflict, but its inscription was later amended to honour the dead of the Second World War as well. Designed by Adrian Jones, an Army veterinary officer serving from 1869 to 1890, the sculpture was installed in 1924 at Stanhope Gate, but was moved to its present site near the bandstand in 1961, following the widening of Park Lane.

rides in the middle just to the right of a Warrant Officer carrying the Sovereign's Standard. When Her Majesty is not resident in London, the Guard is reduced to two NCOs and ten Troopers, commanded by a Corporal of Horse, a rank unique to the Household Cavalry. Whether in the mounted box facing Whitehall, or as dismounted sentries in the archway and the front yard of Horse Guards, the men maintain the protective vigil that connects them to their forebears of 1660.

In addition to its role in The Queen's Birthday Parade when the Household Cavalry Mounted Regiment provides four mounted divisions to escort the Sovereign and perform a March Past, The Life Guards are visible at the Garter Ceremony at Windsor Castle in the dismounted role, lining the route to the chapel for the investiture of new members to the Order. At other times of the year The Life Guards fulfil ceremonial duties at awards and honours investitures, the State Opening of Parliament, State Visits, Remembrance Sunday and the Lord Mayor's Show.

In order to perform at the highest level demanded by such duties, a Trooper's day is long and arduous. After Reveille at 05:30, horses are exercised between 07:00 and 10:00, 365 days a year – horses need constant care and attention, regardless of public holidays. This is followed by painstaking hours of kit and equipment maintenance and cleaning for it to be presented to the most exacting standards required on ceremonial occasions.

THE BLUES AND ROYALS The Blues and Royals were formed in 1969 with the amalgamation of two of the oldest cavalry regiments in the British Army – The Royal Horse Guards, always known as The Blues, and The Royal Dragoons. It was a fitting marriage, as both regiments had fought together many times throughout their long history.

The Blues were originally part of Cromwell's New Model Army, raised by General Monck in 1650, along with the Coldstream Guards, and fought initially in Scotland. They were, perhaps ironically for a regiment who were later to have such strong royal connections, fiercely puritan and were among the most extreme opponents of Parliament. A more moderate Colonel, Unton Croke, gradually weaned them off such radical views and by 1660 Monck regarded them as his most loyal regiment of horse.

Due to be disbanded in 1661, along with most of the army, they were saved after they proved themselves helpful in putting down Venner's rebellion of religious cranks, the Fifth Monarchy Men, and were established in February 1661 as the Royal Regiment of Horse, with Aubrey de Vere, the Earl of Oxford, as their Colonel. In its Parliamentarian incarnation the regiment had worn dark blue coats, and as the Earl's personal livery was also blue the regiment quickly adopted the nickname of The Blues.

The Royal Dragoons, always known as The Royals, were raised soon afterwards to garrison Charles II's new colony of Tangier, part of the dowry of Catherine of Braganza, and endured a hot, uncomfortable and bloody 20 years fighting the Moors. Most of them came from Cromwell's dragoon regiments, soldiers who fought on foot but moved around the battlefield on horses. Tangier is the first Battle Honour to appear on the Standards of The Blues and Royals, and the oldest on any Colours, Standards or Guidons in the British Army.

Returning in 1684, they fought alongside The Blues at Sedgemoor in 1685 under their Colonel John Churchill, the great Duke of Marlborough, to crush the Duke of Monmouth's rebellion. Both regiments then fought side by side in the Jacobite wars in Ireland and in William III's incessant war against France in the Low Countries, one of Britain's bloodiest and most unrewarding conflicts.

Throughout the 18th century both regiments found themselves spending long years on policing and anti-smuggling duties around the British Isles, interspersed with bouts of fighting the French, in the wars of the Spanish and Austrian successions, the Seven Years War, and in the wars against Revolutionary France in the 1790s. At the Battle of Dettingen in 1734 The Royals captured the white satin Standard of the *Mousquetaires Noires* French cavalry, while at the Battle of Warburg in 1760 the Marquess of Granby, the bald colonel of The Blues, earned a lasting place

A Trooper of The Blues and Royals in Dismounted Review Order.

The Princess Royal, Colonel, The Blues and Royals, on The Queen's Birthday Parade in her uniquely adapted Full Dress, riding Elizabeth. She is holding the Gold Stick in her left hand, denoting that at this Queen's Birthday Parade she was on duty as Gold Stick-in-Waiting.

in the regiment's folklore for his decisive role in the battle – and the loss of his wig.

The period after the Seven Years War was a relatively dull one for The Blues, spent on internal policing, although they did much to advance military equitation, building the first military riding school in Nottingham. In 1804 they moved to new barracks in Windsor built by George III on the site of an old leper hospital. Combermere Barracks, as it later became, has been their home ever since. The Blues were a great favourite of the king, who kept them on duty at Windsor Castle for the last 20 years of his reign. 1 January 1813 marked the first step in the elevation of The Blues to the status of Household Cavalry when the Duke of Wellington was made their Colonel. The two regiments would fight together again in the Peninsular War, The Blues serving for a shorter time than The Royals who spent five long years campaigning in Portugal, Spain and France. This was a time of change as the not very efficient British Army that had fought in the Low Countries in the 1790s became, after the Duke of York's reforms and Wellington's leadership, one of the most effective Britain has fielded.

Returning to Britain in 1814, and severely reduced in the aftermath of Napoleon's first exile, both regiments would hurry to Belgium in April 1815 to face the French once more at Waterloo. The Blues, in the Household Brigade, and The Royals in the Union Brigade, distinguished themselves so notably in

the great charge that routed D'Erlon's Corps and destroyed Napoleon's main attack, but it came at a cost: only half The Royals returned.

The Blues' long years of loyal service were recognised when, in 1820, they were granted equal status in the Household Cavalry with the 1st and 2nd regiments of The Life Guards and thus moved from Windsor to Regent's Park Barracks to begin rotational sentry duty at Horse Guards.

The mid-19th century was a time of frustration as Britain remained at peace. The Royals deployed to the Crimea, and took part in the successful Charge of the Heavy Brigade at Inkerman, more often remembered for the less successful effort of their light brigade brethren. The Blues found life in England increasingly boring and it was with relief that Britain's imperial expansion finally allowed them to deploy squadrons to Egypt, Sudan and later as part of a composite Household Cavalry Regiment, to the Boer War. They served for a year, before they had to bow to pressure to return to London to continue ceremonial duties, whilst The Royals served on, forming mobile cavalry columns until 1902.

The First World War was as much a period of sacrifice and tactical frustration for cavalry regiments as it was for the infantry. First deployed with their horses, it soon became apparent that there was little use for cavalry waiting to exploit a breakthrough that never came. The Blues became machine gunners towards

the end of the war, although The Royals remained on horses until the very end, finally getting in the odd charge when the German lines broke in the autumn of 1918. Both regiments took the same terrible casualties as the rest of the Army.

The 1920s were another period of frustration; defence cuts meant that the mechanisation which had ensured victory in 1918 was never pursued, and, although The Royals enjoyed tours in India, 1939 found both regiments part of an army badly unprepared to face Nazi Germany. The learning curve was steep, for The Blues in Palestine, where they deployed for the last time on horses, and for The Royals in North Africa. Soon mechanised, The Blues, again forming a composite Household Cavalry Regiment with The Life Guards, took part in the extraordinary campaign in Syria and Iraq before redeploying to North Africa and fighting at Alamein and then with the 8th Army up through Italy. In 1944 a second Household Cavalry composite regiment deployed on D-Day and fought through France into Germany, taking part in the liberation of Copenhagen in May 1945. A Blues officer, Lieutenant Colonel Robert Laycock, achieved notable distinction as one of the founders of the Commandos. He commanded Special Service Brigade Layforce in the Middle East theatre of operations and became the fifth and last Chief of Combined Operations, taking over from Vice Admiral Lord Louis Mountbatten in 1943 until 1947.

Post-war both regiments served in Germany, on both tanks and armoured cars, and in the operations that marked the drawdown from Empire. The defence cuts of the late 1960s required a reduction in Britain's cavalry, now armoured, forces, and amalgamations were inevitable. The two regiments amalgamated in 1969 to become officially The Royal Horse Guards and 1st Dragoons, but always to be known as The Blues and Royals. The amalgamated regiment deployed to Cyprus, Northern Ireland and sent two troops to the Falklands in 1982 to provide armoured reconaissance.

After the fall of the Iron Curtain in 1989 further Army reductions meant that The Blues and Royals formed two unionised regiments with The Life Guards: a reconnaissance regiment in Windsor and a mounted ceremonial regiment in London. This arrangement has worked remarkably well, harking back to 19th- and 20th-century deployments. The Windsor-based Household Cavalry Regiment has been to the fore of the operations in Bosnia, Kosovo, Iraq and Afghanistan, while the Mounted Regiment has continued the long tradition of immaculate ceremonial. Unton Croke and John Churchill would both have been proud and possibly not a little surprised that the regiments they commanded over three centuries ago now play such a distinguished part in Britain's Armed Forces.

The Blues and Royals share with The Life Guards the unique privilege of

THE CAPLESS SALUTE

Uniquely in the British Army, officers, non-commissioned officers and soldiers of The Blues and Royals are permitted to salute while not wearing headgear. This curious tradition pays tribute to John Manners, Marquess of Granby, who was Colonel of The Blues during the Seven Years War. At the Battle of Warburg on 31 July 1760 the Marquess charged at the head of the British cavalry, losing his hat and wig in the process yet still observing protocol and managing to salute the Commander-in-Chief, Prince Ferdinand of Brunswick. The ferocious charge on the French cavalry caught them in the act of retiring, inflicted considerable losses and drove them across the river with the rest of Lieutenant General Le Chevalier du Muy's troops. The French are said to have suffered between 6,000 and 8,000 casualties, compared to the combined German and British total of 1,200, with cavalry losses described as 'trifling'.

The Marquess has the added distinction of having more British pubs named after him than any other person, as he generously used to establish his old soldiers as publicans – he is depicted wigless on the pub signs.

carrying out mounted and dismounted ceremonial duties, yet little differences remain. The newest officers are called Cornets, not Second Lieutenants; Blues and Royals cross the stirrups over the saddle after dismounting, rather than running them up the leathers, and wear the chinstrap on the chin, rather than the lower lip. While a Life Guard can sometimes be seen gurning furiously to keep a slipping helmet in place, his Blues and Royal opposite number grimaces as his inflexible helmet is pulled down tightly (and irretrievably) over his temples by opening his mouth to give an order.

New recruits undergo what is said to be one of the Army's hardest training courses when they learn to ride and care for horses at the Riding School in Windsor. The vast majority of the soldiers have had no prior experience of horses, and regularly 'being binned' – falling off – is essential to mastering the many skills they will need to serve in the Household Cavalry. As part of the daily routine in London the horses are taken on the early morning ride known as Watering Order, so called as they used to ride out to the many water troughs once scattered around the city. Wormwood Scrubs is a popular destination and the 14-mile round trip provides plenty of exercise for horse and rider before returning to barracks and continuing with the preparations for the regiment's many high-profile ceremonial duties.

THE KING'S TROOP, ROYAL HORSE ARTILLERY

It was the outbreak of war with revolutionary France that prompted the formation of Britain's first two Troops of horse artillery on 1 February 1793 to provide mobile fire support for the cavalry. This gives the Royal Horse Artillery the highest precedence in the British Army, even above its parent unit the Royal Artillery, with only The Life Guards and The Blues and Royals ranking above it.

The development of the 'galloper' or 'grasshopper' gun had meant that a gun could be pulled by one horse between the shafts, so guns could now keep pace with fast-moving troops. The Duke of Richmond and Lennox was Master General of the Ordnance at this time, overseeing the artillery, and he enthusiastically championed the new possibilities offered by horse artillery by summoning 'A' Troop to his family seat at Goodwood for its training. A 'Riding House Department of His Majesty's Ordnance' was then formed by Royal Warrant in 1803, and a German officer, Captain C.A. Quist, appointed as the first Riding Master. Quist, a student of the Spanish Riding School of Vienna, drew on Viennese training methods such as working horses between pillars, as seen in the King's Troop's crest.

During Wellington's Peninsular campaign of 1810–13 the reputation of the Royal Horse Artillery as a *corps d'élite* was firmly established. Sir William Napier, present at the Battle of Fuentes d'Onoro on 5 May 1811, described the action of 'I' Troop, vividly capturing the panache the RHA still displays in its Musical Drive: 'The mass [of French horsemen] was rent asunder and [Captain] Norman Ramsey burst forth sword in hand at the head of his battery, his horses breathing fire, stretched like greyhounds along the plain, the guns bounding behind them like things of no weight, and the mounted gunners followed close, with heads bent low and pointed weapons, in desperate career.'

In 1899 the Royal Artillery was split into two groups, with the Royal Horse Artillery joining the Royal Field Artillery as part of the first group. This arrangement lasted throughout the First World War, which could be called 'the Gunner's War', so central was the role of artillery on both sides. The six Quick Firing 13-pounder guns of today's King's Troop were part of the Army's huge firepower. In 1924 the two groups were reamalgamated into the Royal Artillery. With horses no longer weapons of war, the RHA's batteries served with armoured troops and other artillery units during the Second World War.

King George VI wished to revive the peacetime practice of Royal Salutes fired in Hyde Park by a traditionally dressed and equipped RHA battery. On 17 April 1946, therefore, the Riding Troop was formed as the saluting battery of the Household Troops, the embodiment of the old Riding House Troop that had been disbanded in 1939. When the king visited the Troop at its St John's Wood Barracks the following

A Bombardier from the King's Troop, Royal Horse Artillery, in Full Dress Order (Dismounted). Drivers are mounted on the nearside of a pair of horses and wear a leg iron on the right boot as protection.

Honorary Colonel of the King's Troop, Royal Horse Artillery, Major General Matthew Sykes CVO riding Jack.

year, he crossed out 'Riding' and wrote 'King's' while signing the visitors' book in the Officers' Mess. The Queen, as Captain General of the Royal Artillery, chose not to change the name to 'Queen's Troop' out of respect for her father, and this special bond between the monarch and the King's Troop continues, strengthened by their shared affection for horses.

The 130 Irish Draught horses range in colour from the light bays of 'A' Subsection to the cavalry blacks of 'F' Sub section, which pull the gun carriage for State funerals. They last performed this duty for the funeral of Baroness Thatcher on 17 April 2013. When the Troop provided the gun carriage for the ceremony of the interment of the Unknown Soldier at Westminster Abbey on 11 November 1920, some of the black horses in the team had seen action in the First World War.

Two of the Troop's war horses are particularly remembered: Jones and Joubert were the lead pair of the gun from 'J' Battery that fired the first shell of the war. They were in harness together throughout, and when they returned to Aldershot in 1919 they were let loose on the square to see where they would go. They made straight for their pre-war stalls. The pair were last on parade at the unveiling of the Gunner Memorial at Hyde Park Corner in 1925, after which they were bought by an RHA officer and retired to his farm.

The Adjutant 'Banging the tail'. The tail is cut a fist's length below the chestnut. There is a story that officers cut the tails because when horsehair was a valuable commodity they wanted to ensure they pocketed the profits from selling it.

The statuette of Jones is very precious to the regiment. It resides in the centre of the Officers' Mess table and goes with them from Woolwich to Wellington Barracks when the Troop is fulfilling ceremonial and public duties. It even goes to Ascot and is placed on the table when the officers have lunch in No. 1 car park.

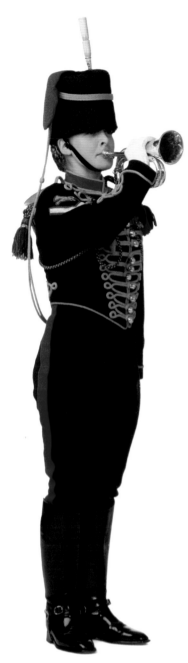

There are approximately 20 trumpet calls for commands. The trumpeters are not musicians, but learn to play while they are Gunners. The officer rides in front of the gun teams, and nods to give the trumpeter the commands.

THE KING'S TROOP JOINING THE REVIEW

In 1997 I had not been sitting at the Great Duke's desk in Horse Guards for long before I received a letter from that oracle of The Queen's Birthday Parade, General Sir Mike Gow. 'How kind of him to write,' I said to the Brigade Major. 'He writes every year after the Troop. What else does he say?' Alexander Matheson nervously enquired. The 'What Else' took up a great deal of time over the next year.

Mike Gow took a passionate interest in the parade and his letter contained a number of proposals. The one that caught my eye was that the King's Troop, Royal Horse Artillery should appear on Horse Guards, rather than merely for the salute in Green Park. I knew the Troop well and felt they were rather out of the public vision.

I was also aware that the Royal Tournament was on borrowed time and the threat of a reduction or disbandment was ever present. So, maybe this idea might work. The Brigade Major was doubtful and the Silver Stick distinctly opposed. But this was not in my gift so I went to see the Senior Colonel, Prince Philip. He advised that I quietly research how it might work and come back with a draft plan.

So after consultations with the King's Troop, Royal Parks and the Police, I sent HRH an outline of how we might include the Troop on the parade. The Troop would arrive via Birdcage Walk and take up a position to the right of the Guards Memorial. Owing to the length of the sub sections or gun teams and in order not to encroach on the grass they would line up in echelon. All mounted troops would therefore be formed up in line along the back of the parade.

The Troop would rank past in pairs of sub sections in advance of the Sovereign's Escort, a proposal which drew exclamations of disdain from the Household Cavalry. After the trot past the Troop would go up the Horse Guards Approach Road and wait for the Queen Mother's carriage returning to the Palace.

The officers would go to the rear of the Troop and face Horse Guards so they could salute at the conclusion of the parade. Then after the signal that the Queen Mother was clear the Troop would trot down The Mall to take up position around the Queen Victoria Memorial ready to rank past The Queen. They would then move to Green Park and fire the salute at 13:00 as opposed to the normal 11:00.

Prince Philip replied promptly; we should progress the planning and pay particular attention to timings in order that the parade was not unduly lengthened. The introduction of the Troop added just one minute to its length, but it meant the Troop had a longer day, not getting back to barracks until after 14:00.

After the early morning rehearsal for mounted troops we changed our minds on how the Troop should form up. The echelon arrangement looked odd so we reverted to the idea of encroaching on the grass so that the sub sections were square to the parade, and we placed the Mounted Band in the centre.

The next step was to present the proposal to Her Majesty and this I did on my hands and knees with a scale plan showing how the Troop would move through the parade. The Queen approved in principle but her Private Secretary made it plain that the responsibility for the success of this venture was mine. Given the murmurings from some senior quarters not only was I worried but I was also determined that it should work.

All was set for the great day. But there was one other hurdle. Every year the evening before the parade the Senior Colonel holds a meeting in Buckingham Palace for the Colonels of the Household Division, which the Major General briefs. I concluded with a brief on the King's Troop's inclusion. I then held my breath as I knew the two Gold Sticks wanted to express their views; if they were the first to speak I expected others to voice doubts. In the event the Senior Colonel invited The Prince of Wales to comment. He said that if his grandfather were alive he would be absolutely delighted; so that was that and everyone assented.

The next day passed off well, the Troop looked immaculate and the general view was that it was a thoroughly good addition to the parade. More to the point The Queen was pleased.

There was, however, one issue. The firing of the salute at 13:00 coincided untidily with the flypast. After considering alternatives such as going back to 11:00 which meant the Troop could not arrive on time at the start of the parade, we plumped for 12:52, which, with the seven minutes it takes to fire the salute, allows a minute between the end of the salute and the flypast.

The last word should come from the oracle himself, General Mike Gow, who wrote to me expressing his delight that at least I had listened to one of his ideas.

But the letters did not stop!

By Major General Sir Evelyn Webb-Carter

THE GRENADIER GUARDS The Grenadier Guards are the oldest of
the five Regiments of Foot Guards. They came into being as a recognisable unit in
1656 composed from exiles loyal to Charles II, who had fled to the Continent after
his father's execution and his own defeat in the Battle of Worcester. Charles raised a
regiment in Bruges from among his supporters, and named it the 'Royal Regiment
of Guards'. They fought under the command of Lord Wentworth against Cromwell
at the Battle of the Dunes, near Dunkirk, on 28 May 1658. Charles had allied himself to Philip IV of Spain, whose privateers were using Dunkirk as a base for attacks
on English shipping, in the hope that Spain would support a Royalist invasion of
England. Louis XV invoked a treaty he had made with the Commonwealth and be-
sieged Dunkirk with the help of Cromwellian regiments. Under General Turenne's
command, they beat off the Spanish and Royalist army that tried to raise the siege,
and entered Dunkirk. The survivors of Wentworth's Royal Regiment of Guards
served on in Flanders.

On 23 November 1660, Charles II, restored to his throne but doubting the loyalty
of the Army he found in England, commissioned Colonel John Russell to raise a new
'King's Regiment of Foot Guards', consisting of 12 companies, the first of which
was named the King's Company. In 1664 Wentworth's regiment was recalled to
England and, after its Colonel's death the following year, was combined with Russell's regiment, with an establishment of 24 companies. In 1672 one of these fought as
marines in the Battle of Solebay against the Dutch; the brave conduct of one of the
Foot Guards ensigns, John Churchill, so impressed the Lord Admiral, the Duke of
York, that he made Churchill a Captain in his own regiment: the first promotion of
perhaps the greatest British soldier, the Duke of Marlborough.

By 1685 the regiment was known as the First Regiment of Foot Guards. Around
this time the companies were organised into battalions, which became the usual tactical unit throughout the infantry. From the early 1700s onwards, the regiment had
three battalions. In 1815 the 3rd Battalion played a pivotal role in the final defeat of
Napoleon at Waterloo. The Light Company supported the 2nd Battalions of the 2nd
and 3rd Guards defending the farm and château of Hougoumont, by holding the
orchard against the day-long attacks of the corps led by Napoleon's brother Jerome.
Later the whole of the 3rd Battalion played a central part in Major General Maitland's 1st Guards Brigade when it routed the final advance of the hitherto unbeaten
French Imperial Guard.

Since the 17th century, the elite infantry in most European armies were the Grenadiers, the tallest and strongest men, chosen to carry and throw grenades. By the time
of the Napoleonic Wars, each British infantry battalion's senior company was its
Grenadier company, distinguished by white plumes in its headdress; in Napoleon's

*Captain, Grenadier
Guards, in Guard of
Honour Order, denoted
by his gold sash and
sword knot.*

The Duke of York, 26th Colonel, Grenadier Guards, in Guard of Honour Order. Photographed in Windsor Castle

Imperial Guard, the elite of the elite were Grenadier regiments, distinguished by their huge bearskin caps. It was these regiments that the First Regiment of Foot Guards routed at Waterloo; they were given their title and their headdress in commemoration, becoming the 'First or Grenadier Regiment of Foot Guards', which remains their proper name. They still wear the white plumes and, regardless of what order of dress Grenadier Guardsmen are wearing, their cap badge is a 'grenade fired proper' with 17 flames. It is polished twice a day, as it is made from brass and a tarnished grenade is frowned upon. The privilege of wearing the bearskin cap was extended to the other regiments of Foot Guards in 1832.

Waterloo took its place among the Honorary Distinctions, or Battle Honours, of the regiment. These now total 74, of which 45 are currently borne on the Colours, the consecrated flags that were originally carried in battle to act as rallying points, and, still embodying the fighting spirit of each regiment, are treasured and paraded on special occasions to commemorate and inspire. The Grenadier Guards remember Waterloo in other ways too; for instance, they march across Hyde Park Corner at attention, recalling the fact that they always adopted that posture to salute the Duke of Wellington when he lived there, in Apsley House (No. 1, London).

Four members of the 3rd Battalion Grenadier Guards were among the first recipients of the Victoria Cross for their

There are 13 ties around the sword basket denoting the 13 Victoria Crosses won by the regiment. The 14th was awarded posthumously to Lance Corporal James Ashworth in 2013, for exceptional bravery in action in Helmand Province, Afghanistan.

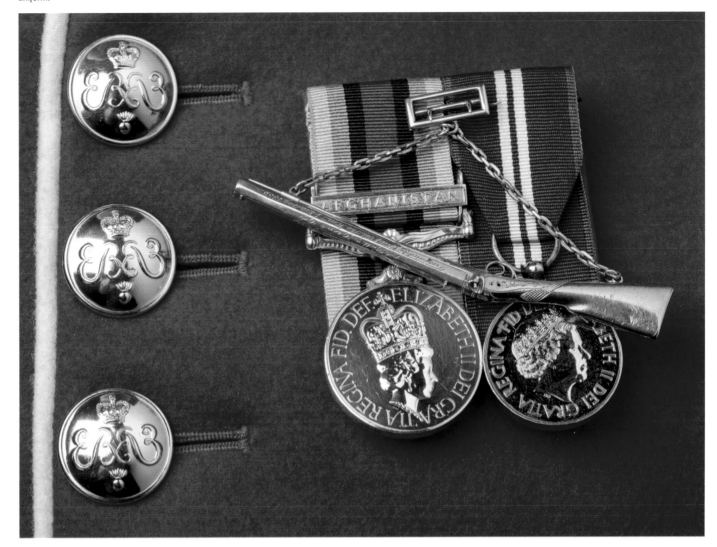

The gold rifle is awarded to the best shot in the Grenadier Guards and can be worn on their uniform.

valour in Crimea, three of them at the Battle of Inkerman. Battalions fought in Egypt and South Africa, and then in France and Flanders during the Great War, joined by the 4th Battalion raised in 1914 and the 5th Battalion in 1915. Both were disbanded in 1919. A further seven Victoria Crosses were awarded to Grenadiers during the Great War.

The regiment reached its maximum size in the Second World War: the 4th Battalion was re-formed in 1940 as an armoured (tank) battalion, fighting in north-west Europe from D-Day until 1945 in 6th Guards Tank Brigade. The 5th Battalion was re-formed in 1941 along with a 6th Battalion, both fighting in North Africa and Italy. These three battalions were disbanded at the end of the war, during which two more Victoria Crosses were won by Grenadiers.

Since 1945 the regiment has served in Germany, Palestine, Egypt, Libya, Malaysia, Cyprus, British Cameroon, British Guyana, Kenya, Northern Ireland, Bosnia, Kosovo, Iraq and Afghanistan. Captain Robert Nairac won the George Cross posthumously in Northern Ireland; Lance Corporal James Ashworth became the 14th Grenadier to win the Victoria Cross, in Afghanistan in 2012.

The 3rd Battalion was placed in suspended animation in 1961; its customs and spirit live on in the Inkerman Company in the 1st Battalion. Defence cuts after the end of the Cold War placed the 2nd Battalion in suspended animation in 1992; its Colours, spirit and customs survive in the Nijmegen Company, the senior of three companies of Foot Guards dedicated to Public Duties. Nijmegen Company is based in Wellington Barracks, and a soldier passing out of basic training will be posted to this company to learn how to be a 'proper Grenadier' for six to nine months. Afterwards he will usually be posted to the 1st Battalion for a bout of 'green soldiering' at its base in Aldershot.

Through all these changes, the core purpose of guarding the Sovereign, and the ancient structural building block of the regiment, has remained, exemplified in the First or Grenadier Regiment of Foot Guards by their motto: 'Honi soit qui mal y pense' – 'Evil be to him who evil thinks'. Its ancient royal origin reminds all Guardsmen of their duty and loyalty to the Sovereign, and the fundamental respect for others that underpins all they do. And the senior company of the regiment is still the Sovereign's – currently The Queen's Company – as it was when Charles II raised the regiment in 1660.

THE COLDSTREAM GUARDS In 1645, Oliver Cromwell formed the New Model Army, the first professional standing army in Britain. He expanded it in 1650 to oppose Charles II's threatened invasion from Scotland and commissioned General George Monck to raise new regiments of horse and foot. Monck formed his infantry regiment by taking five companies each from George Fenwick's and Sir Arthur Haselrig's regiments, with the new Monck's Regiment of Foot being officially formed on 23 August 1650. They fought their first battle less than a fortnight later, contributing to Cromwell's victory over Leslie's Royalists in the Battle of Dunbar. The new regiment was left in a force 5,000 strong, commanded by their Colonel, to subjugate Scotland, while Cromwell pursued Charles II to defeat him at Worcester.

After Cromwell's death in 1658 and the abdication of his son Richard, General Monck, opposed to the political ambitions and strong Presbyterianism of his fellow Generals, marched his regiment south to London from the border town of Cold-stream on 1 January 1660 to help secure the restoration of the monarchy. They took up quarters in St James's on 2 February, and were employed in keeping order in the City of London. Their intervention was instrumental in enabling Charles II to return to take up his throne in May 1660. Monck was rewarded with a dukedom, the Order of the Garter, the star of which his regiment adopted as its cap star, and the title of Lord General (the equivalent of Commander-in-Chief).

The new regime decided to disband the New Model Army, but in January 1661, before the Act of Parliament to do so could be promulgated, Parliament had to call on Monck and his regiment to deal with the rebellion of the Fifth Monarchy Men, religious radicals led by Thomas Venner, who had declared a divinely led republic. King Charles gratefully decided to retain Monck's, now called the Lord General's, Regiment, but to comply with the Act of Parliament, they were paraded at the Tower of London on 14 February 1661, ordered to lay down their arms, and then immediately to take them up again as soldiers of the king, 'an extraordinary Guard to his Royal person', with the official title 'the Lord General's Foot Guards'. They thus became the 2nd Regiment of Foot Guards in the new English Army, despite them arguing that they had originally been raised some years before the 1st Regiment (now the Grenadiers). To make this point they adopted the motto 'Nulli Secundus' ('Second to None'). They remained 'the Lord General's Foot Guards' until Monck's death in 1670, when they were officially given the name they had borne colloquially for a decade: the Coldstream Regiment of Foot Guards.

Since then the regiment has served in almost every campaign of the British Army, amassing an extraordinary total of 117 Honorary Distinctions or Battle Honours. The first is Tangier, where in 1680 a composite battalion of 1st and Coldstream Guards fought as marine infantry, successfully attacking the Moors who were besieging the

A Company Sergeant Major of the Coldstream Guards presenting arms with the SA80 assault rifle.

Lieutenant General Sir James Bucknall, 29th Colonel, Coldstream Guards, wearing Frock Coat Order, which is uniquely an 'Undress' uniform that can be worn (with the Breast Star and one neck decoration) on any Full Dress occasion.

English garrison and population from the sea. This was not the regiment's first experience as marines; 50 members had earlier joined one of their officers, Sir Robert Holmes, who was a Royal Navy officer as well as holding a commission in the Coldstream, in his 1664 expedition to Guinea and America, where he captured New Amsterdam and renamed it New York. The regiment took part in capturing New York again, in a composite Foot Guards Battalion, in 1776, during the American Revolutionary War, and served in the occupation of Washington in 1814.

A silver statuette of a Coldstream Guards musketeer.

Among the regiment's many Battle Honours, none is more important than Waterloo, where the 2nd Battalion played a crucial role in the defence of the château and farm of Hougoumont. Napoleon had ordered his troops to seize the Duke of Wellington's strategic position on the Mont St Jean Ridge, not far from Brussels. Hougoumont, with its dozen buildings, was situated in woodland directly below the position Wellington chose to stop the French infantry's advance.

In his Despatch the Iron Duke wrote that the post at Hougoumont 'was maintained throughout the day with the utmost gallantry by these brave troops notwithstanding the repeated efforts of large bodies of the enemy to obtain possession of it'. Wellington nominated Corporal James Graham for an annual annuity of £10, offered by John Norcross, Rector of Framlingham. Graham, a 24-year-old Irishman in the Coldstream, had assisted his commanding officer, Lieutenant Colonel James Macdonnell, in closing the gates at Hougoumont. This pivotal incident is commemorated every year in the ceremony of 'Hanging the Brick', in which an original brick from Hougoumont is paraded through the barracks with the honour due to the Colours, and then ceremoniously hung in the Sergeants' Mess, and Graham's and others exploits at Waterloo celebrated.

When in 1832 the honour of wearing the bearskin cap to commemorate the Foot Guards' defeat of Napoleon's

Oliver Cromwell on the reverse side of the Dunbar Medal from 1650.

Imperial Guard at the culmination of Waterloo was extended to all three regiments, the Coldstream wore red plumes (the traditional colour of British infantry line companies) in the right side of theirs. This was to make them readily identifiable in their customary position on the left of the Foot Guards line of battle. They retained their traditional white bands on their forage caps, from which they received their nickname 'the Lilywhites'.

Four members of the regiment won the newly instituted Victoria Cross for their valour in the Crimean War, and in 1855 the regiment received its current official title, the Coldstream Guards. The 3rd Battalion was raised in 1897; both 1st and 2nd Battalions served in the South African War. All three battalions fought in the First World War, during which the 4th (Pioneer) Battalion was raised, joining the other three in France

in 1915. It was disbanded in 1919, but re-formed in 1940 to fight as an Armoured (tank) Battalion as part of 6th Guards Tank Brigade in north-west Europe during the Second World War. The 5th Battalion was formed in 1941, to fight as a Motorised Battalion in the Guards Armoured Division; it was disbanded in 1945, but not before some playing the roles of soldiers being evacuated from Dunkirk in Noël Coward's 1942 film *In Which We Serve*. A 6th Battalion was also raised in late 1941, but was disbanded in 1943 without seeing action.

Since the two world wars, in which Coldstream Guardsmen won a further nine Victoria Crosses, battalions of the regiment have served in Germany, Palestine, Egypt, Tripoli, Malaya, Cyprus, Aden, Kuwait, Mauritius, Zanzibar, Libya, British Guyana, British Honduras, Northern Ireland, the Gulf, Bosnia, Iraq and Afghanistan. The 3rd Battalion was placed in suspended animation in 1959, and in a further round of defence cuts the 2nd Battalion followed it in 1992, leaving its Colours, customs and spirit to live on in a Public Duties Incremental Company, Number 7 Company. Based at Wellington Barracks, its primary role is guarding royal palaces and providing State Ceremonial. Generally, soldiers spend between three and nine months in Number 7 Company, following their Combat Infantryman's Course at the Infantry Training Centre Catterick and before being posted to the 1st Battalion in Windsor. The company maintains its military skills, with regular training exercises outside London and overseas adventure training.

The Coldstream Guards' motto 'Nulli secundus' perfectly summarises the excellence Guardsmen demand of themselves in all they do. It also recalls the fact that they are one of the only two regiments that were in the New Model Army (the other being The Blues and Royals), making them the two oldest with unbroken service in the British Army.

FAMILY REGIMENTS

Each regiment in the British Army is more than a professional organisation trained to fight The Queen's enemies and defend her friends. Each one prides itself in delivering the military covenant – the commitment between the nation and every member of the Armed Forces that, in return for the individual soldier's unlimited liability ultimately to give their life in the course of their duties, they and their families can expect to be looked after by the nation.

For most soldiers, for most of their service, the regiment is both job and home; the organisation which means that there is no 'work/life balance' in the regular Army, because the profession of arms is the soldier's life, lived on the closest terms, often in conditions of great stress and danger, with the fellow members of the regiment whom you trust with your life. From when the soldier joins, the regiment provides for every need. Its association and charitable funds play a great part in the life of all its members (and their families) who call upon them, long after they retire; indeed to the grave and beyond: after the regimental funerals which many request, widows and orphans receive all kinds of help, and above all the hand of friendship. This

is what we mean when we call ourselves family regiments, and say 'Once a Grenadier (Coldstreamer, Scots or Welsh Guardsman, or Mick) always a…'

We also pride ourselves on the numbers of families whose members serve among us for generations. The ten generations of Tollemaches in the Coldstream Guards make them indeed 'Nulli Secundus' ('Second to None'), but every regiment in the Household Division can boast of families whose names appear again and again. Guardsmen all know examples, such as the two Generals in one regiment, father and son, who lost the same leg in successive world wars, while commanding platoons in the same battalion; the three brothers who served together in another regiment in the Falklands, and all achieved warrant or commissioned rank; the photograph of 11 officers serving together in another battalion, all with their fathers who had preceded them in the same regiment. The examples are legion; more important is the fact that, whether related or not, we are all brothers and sisters in arms.

Captain Tom Tollemache pictured alongside his ancestor and namesake, Lieutenant General Thomas Talmash, who died after wounds received at the Battle of Camaret in 1694 leading an expedition against the French port of Brest in the Nine Years War. The Lieutenant General was the third Colonel of the Coldstream Guards and started the family connection to the regiment when he joined as a Captain in 1678. Captain Tom Tollemache is the 10th and most recent generation of the family to have served in the Coldstream Guards and was the Assistant Equerry to The Queen and Regimental Recruiting Officer.

THE SCOTS GUARDS The Scots Guards are rightly proud of being the oldest regiment in the Foot Guards, though the third in seniority. Their history mirrors the complicated history of the creation of the United Kingdom. On 16 March 1642 King Charles I commissioned Archibald, 1st Marquis of Argyle, to raise in Scotland a regiment of 1,500 men for service in Ulster, where the Irish were rebelling against the Scottish colonists. The king intended to command these operations himself, and Arglye's Regiment was to be his 'Life Guard of Foot'. However, events in England thwarted this plan, and the regiment deployed to Ulster under the command of Argyle's kinsman, Sir Duncan Campbell of Auchinbreck, whose commission, along with Argyle's, is still preserved in the Regimental Headquarters in Wellington Barracks.

In the turmoil of the English Civil War in the mid-1640s, the regiment, now known as 'the Irish Companies', returned to Scotland and fought against the Royalist commander, James Graham, 1st Marquis of Montrose. In 1650, however, when Charles II made his way to Scotland to carry on the fight after his father's execution, Argyle's Regiment became his Life Guard of Foot, under the command of Argyle's son, Lord Lorne. They received their first Colours at Falkland Palace, and fought in the Royalist defeats at Dunbar and Worcester, which resulted in Charles's flight into exile on the Continent. Scotland was conquered by Cromwell, and the Life Guard of Foot scattered.

After his Restoration Charles II turned his attention back to Scotland and in October 1660 issued orders for the re-raising of companies of Scottish Foot Guards to garrison the castles of Edinburgh and Dumbarton. In 1662 these companies were expanded into a regiment, and the Earl of Linlithgow appointed its third Colonel. In 1694 seven companies of the regiment came south to Hounslow Heath to be brigaded with the other two Regiments of Foot Guards for the first time.

King William III ruled that their precedence in the Foot Guards should date from 1686, when they had first been brought into the establishment of the English Army. They became known to the English as the Scotch or Scots Guards, and, rumour has it, to their fellow Foot Guards, teasingly, as 'the Kiddies'. They took their place in the centre of the Foot Guards line of battle, between the 1st and Coldstream Regiments.

About the time of the Act of Union in 1707, the regiment took the star of the Most Ancient and Most Noble Order of the Thistle (founded in 1687 by King James II and VII) as their cap star, and its motto 'Nemo Me Impune Lacessit' ('No One Provokes Me with Impunity') as their own.

Queen Anne officially renamed the regiment the 3rd Regiment of Foot Guards in 1711. In about 1774 the regiment started wearing their buttons in groups of three, to distinguish them from the 1st Guards' single buttons, and the Coldstream's pairs.

A Scots Guards Sergeant in Guard Order, standing easy.

The Duke of Kent, 25th
Colonel, Scots Guards
in Service dress. His
Forage Cap belonged
to his grandfather,
George V. The stars on
the Duke's shoulder are
small representations
of the star of Scotland's
senior order of chivalry,
the Order of the
Thistle. Service Dress
is almost unchanged
since the uniforms
worn by officers in the
First World War, which
became established
uniform soon afterwards.
The cloth is called
Guards Baratea and
became the basis for
the officers' uniforms
of other regiments
that emerged from
the provenance of the
Guards Division, such as
the Parachute Regiment.

A silver statuette of a Scots Guards piper.

The regiment distinguished itself in all the major 18th-century campaigns of the British Army, as well as in security duties in London. In 1780 it provided a detachment to guard the Bank of England during the Gordon Riots; this guard, known as 'the Bank Picquet', remained a routine duty of the Foot Guards in London until 1973.

The regiment participated in virtually every major action of the Napoleonic Wars – in Portugal, Spain and the Low Countries. Among its many Battle Honours, one of the greatest was Waterloo, where the 2nd Battalion defended Hougoumont with 2nd Battalion Coldstream Guards in 2nd Guards Brigade. In 1832 the honour of wearing the bearskin cap in commemoration of the defeat of Napoleon's Imperial Guard was extended to the regiment, worn with no plume (reflecting their position in the centre of the Foot Guards line of battle). In 1831 the regiment was redesignated the Scots Fusilier Guards; in 1877 Queen Victoria restored the title Scots Guards.

By then four members of the regiment had won the newly instituted Victoria Cross for their valour in saving the Colours at the Battle of the Alma in September 1854, during which the regiment won three more Battle Honours. Two months later, in the chaos of the Battle of Inkerman, 1st Battalion drove off the superior forces of Russian infantry with desperate bayonet charges over six long hours. Victoria instituted the supreme gallantry award which bears her name in 1857, with the order being backdated to 1854 in order to recognise acts of valour during the Crimean War. Captain Robert Lindsay, one of the four Scots Fusilier Guards recipients, was the first British soldier actually to receive the decoration, when the queen awarded the first 62 in person in Hyde Park on 26 June 1857. The *London Gazette* described his actions: 'When the formation of the line of the Regiment was disordered at Alma, Captain Lindsay stood firm with the Colours, and by his example and energy, greatly tended to restore order. At Inkerman, at a most trying moment, he, with a few men, charged a party of Russians, driving them back, and running one through the body himself.'

Both 1st and 2nd Battalions Scots Guards were engaged in the South African War of 1899–1902, and on 3 January 1911 a detachment provided support to the police in the Siege of Sidney Street in the East End of London. In the First World War, 111 officers and 2,730 other ranks gave their lives. The 3rd (Reserve) Battalion was raised in August 1914; it was disbanded in March 1919, but reformed in October 1940, becoming a Tank Battalion in the Guards Armoured Division. The 4th Battalion was formed in September 1941, but disbanded in October 1943. The 5th (Ski) Battalion had an even shorter life: it was raised on 6 February 1940 to serve in Finland when that country was invaded by Russia, but when the Finns capitulated on 14 March, the volunteers who had joined it from across the Brigade of Guards returned to their parent units and the battalion faded out of existence.

Another Scots Guards innovation of the Second World War has had a longer and most remarkable history: the Special Air Service. The SAS was raised and commanded by David Stirling, who had been commissioned into the Scots Guards in 1937. He joined Lieutenant Colonel Robert Laycock's 8 (Guards) Commando in 1940, one of the original Commandos, which were all army units; the Royal Marines were tasked to raise nine further Commandos from 1942 onwards. Stirling raised and led the first SAS unit in North Africa; many of the other founding members of the new regiment were also members of the Household Cavalry or Foot Guards.

Another Scots Guardsman, Captain Lord Lyell, was awarded the Victoria Cross posthumously in Tunisia in 1943, the 11th won by members of the regiment. Accompanied by a Sergeant, a Lance Corporal and two Guardsmen, he led an attack on an enemy post consisting of an 88mm gun and a heavy machine gun. He killed the machine gun crew in one pit with a hand grenade and then, with cover only from the Lance Corporal, the other men having become casualties, he leapt into the second pit and killed several of the crew before losing his own life. Both the guns had been silenced. Losses during the Second World War amounted to 98 officers and 943 other ranks.

The regiment's tercentenary fell in 1942, in the middle of the war, which precluded any significant celebration. A special programme about the regiment was broadcast on the BBC, however, and a historical pageant was enacted at the depot at Pirbright, while the 2nd Battalion was granted a day's holiday in the Western Desert.

Since 1945 battalions of the Scots Guards have served in Malaya, Cyprus, Egypt, Germany, Kenya, Malaysia, Borneo, Northern Ireland, Hong Kong (China), Sierra Leone, Iraq and Afghanistan. The 2nd Battalion was placed in suspended animation in March 1971 but reconstituted at Edinburgh in January 1972; it added further fame and another Battle Honour (now totalling 90) to the regiment's history in the Falkland Islands, defeating the Argentinians at Mount Tumbledown, with one of the few post-war bayonet charges in the history of the British Army. The battalion was placed in suspended animation again in November 1993; its spirit, customs and Colours are carried by F Company, which carries out public duties from Wellington Barracks. The Scots Guards are the only Foot Guards regiment in which companies use the traditional letter, rather than numerical designations. The Scots Guards also retain the old usage of Right and Left Flank Companies: traditionally the most vulnerable positions in a battalion's order of battle, these were positions of honour.

In 2015 the 1st Battalion relocated from Catterick to Mons Barracks in Aldershot, as part of a large relocation exercise to accommodate thousands of troops returning from Germany.

Scots Guards Pipe Major James Riddell composed 'The Crags of Tumbledown Mountain' on a cardboard ration pack soon after taking part in the decisive Battle of Mount Tumbledown in the Falkland Islands in 1982. When the desperate battle was won, he sat down to write a quick march to honour his dead comrades, particularly Drill Sergeant Danny White, and played it on the hard-won summit. On the reverse of the pack, he described the events of that night:

'On 14th June 1982, as leading element of the 5th Infantry Brigade attack on ground surrounding Port Stanley, the 2nd Battalion Scots Guards carried out a night attack against troops of the 5th Argentinian Marine Battalion, dug in on the key defensive position of Mt Tumbledown. Fierce fighting ensued for 5 hours before the enemy were finally driven from the feature. Hours after the capture of Mt Tumbledown, the Argentinian resolve failed and all their forces in the Falkland Islands surrendered. Some days after the final surrender, the Argentinian military Governor admitted that with the loss of Mt Tumbledown, he lost any hope of holding on to his positions and was left with no option but to order his troops to lay down their weapons. This tune was written in memory of the nine Scots Guardsmen lost during the Battle for Tumbledown Mountain.'

Later that year the Pipes and Drums of the 2nd Battalion Scots Guards and the Regimental Band of the Scots Guards recorded the tune as a single, donating the proceeds to the Scots Guards Charitable Funds. Pipe Major Riddell was photographed for the cover on the crags themselves.

The first time 'Crags' was played on the parade was in 1995 when the 1st Battalion Scots Guards Colour was trooped.

THE IRISH GUARDS The tunic buttons arranged in fours, the shamrock on the collar and the St Patrick's blue plume on the right side of their bearskins denote the Irish Guards, the fourth regiment of the Foot Guards.

On 1 April 1900 a new Army Order was published: 'Her Majesty The Queen, having deemed it desirable to commemorate the bravery shown by the Irish Regiments in the operations in South Africa in the years 1899 and 1900, has been graciously pleased to command that an Irish Regiment of Foot Guards be formed, to be designated the "Irish Guards".'

This sets the Irish Guards apart as the only British Army regiment raised to honour the gallantry of a nation's soldiers. Irishmen have served with distinction in all Britain's wars: the first ever Victoria Cross was won by Charles Lucas, a Mate on HMS *Hecla*, who was from County Monaghan, as was Corporal James Graham of the Coldstream Guards, whom the Duke of Wellington nominated as the Army's bravest man at Waterloo.

An Irish brigade served the kings of France in the 17th and 18th centuries; one of its regiments had been raised by Charles II in 1662 as his 'Regiment of Foot Guards in Ireland'. Loyal to its Stuart king it accompanied James II into exile in France, and fought in the French service in its scarlet uniform until the French Revolution, when its survivors returned to serve in the British Army. The regiment had taken part in the defeat of the British at Fontenoy in 1745, capturing a Colour, and even fought on British soil as part of the French contingent at Culloden. When the Irish Guards were raised in 1900 no connection was made to the earlier regiment, although many of its soldiers still come from Ireland: a reminder of the important fact that the nationals of many foreign countries serve in the Foot Guards, and indeed throughout the Armed Forces.

At its creation there was much interest in the new regiment; in a letter to *The Times* one correspondent suggested that it should wear orange tunics and green trousers. Thankfully, it was decided that the uniform should be consistent with the rest of the brigade, with its St Patrick's blue plume worn on the right side of the bearskin, as it took its place on the left of the Scots Guards, next to the Coldstream in their traditional place on the left of the line. St Patrick's blue was selected because blue is the colour of the mantle and sash of the Order of St Patrick from which the regiment also takes its cap star and motto. The first plume was made by Lady Settrington, whose husband was Aide-de-Camp to the first Colonel of the regiment, Field Marshal Lord Roberts. At Lord Roberts's behest, she dipped her husband's white Grenadier plume into blue ink. The original plume is still preserved in the Guards Museum in Wellington Barracks. The new regiment was christened 'Bob's Own' after their Colonel, the most revered soldier of his time. More recently they have

A Regimental Quartermaster Sergeant Major of the Irish Guards in Guard Order.

The Duke of Cambridge, 10th Colonel, Irish Guards, in Guard of Honour Order during the Inspection on Horse Guards Parade riding Wellesley. He is the first member of the British Royal Family to hold the Colonelcy, although a recent holder of the office was both royal and a Head of State. The Grand Duke of Luxembourg was made Colonel of the regiment after his service with the Irish Guards during the liberation of Europe, and his own country, in 1945.

A silver statuette of an Irish Guards drummer.

The Queen Mother's pipe banner. Queen Elizabeth the Queen Mother was never Colonel of the Irish Guards, but she presented the regiment she called 'my Micks' with shamrock for nearly 50 years and chose them to bear her coffin.

Honour, 'Mons', in 1914; by the end of the Great War another 29 had been added, along with four Victoria Crosses. The cost is recorded in a booklet that is presented to each officer on joining the regiment: 'The strength of the Regiment on mobilisation in 1914 was 997. During the Great War 293 officers and 9,430 other ranks served as Irish Guardsmen. Of this number 115 officers and 2,235 other ranks gave their lives and a further 195 officers and 5,541 other ranks were wounded. These numbers do not add up because many were wounded once but returned only to be wounded again and these are counted separately.'

These numbers include members of the 2nd Battalion, which was raised in July 1915, disbanded in March 1919, only to be reformed in April 1939; the 3rd Battalion was raised in October 1941.

The 1st Battalion saw its first action and won its first Battle Honour of the Second World War in 1940 in Norway as part of 24th Guards Brigade. Most of the battalion's senior officers and many other ranks were killed when the ship transporting them was bombed.

The 2nd Battalion embarked for the Hook of Holland in May of the same year. Having safeguarded the evacuation of the Dutch Royal Family and Government, the battalion was sent to Boulogne with 2nd Battalion Welsh Guards to buy time for the evacuation of the main body of the British Expeditionary Force from Dunkirk. They fought against overwhelming odds for three days; Navy

become universally and affectionately known as 'the Micks'.

Members of the new regiment were in action in South Africa within months, one officer and 32 other ranks forming a section in the composite Guards Mounted Infantry Company. They returned home in 1902, the same year that the 1st Battalion received its first Colours from Edward VII during the King's Birthday Parade. They won their first Battle

destroyers took off many of the survivors, but both battalions lost nearly 200 men each, killed, wounded or missing. They were both awarded their first Battle Honour of the Second World War, 'Boulogne 1940'.

The following year the 2nd Battalion re-equipped as a tank battalion in the newly formed Guards Armoured Division, where it was joined by the 3rd Battalion, in the infantry role, in 1943: they trained and operated as an integrated Irish Guards armoured battle group for the rest of the war. The 1st Battalion

embarked for North Africa in early 1943, suffering very heavy casualties in several battles, including Djebel Bou Aoukaz, where Lance Corporal John Keneally won the Victoria Cross. It fought on in Italy, where at Anzio its losses were so great that in April 1944 it returned to England and took no further part in the fighting in Europe as a battalion.

The 3rd Battalion was involved in the Normandy landings, arriving in Arromanches on 23 June 1944. Among its advance party was a certain 23-year-old Captain, Jean, Grand Duke of Luxembourg, Prince of Nassau, who had left his Canadian exile to join the Irish Guards on the advice of George VI. During his training he had guarded Buckingham Palace and had to remain silent while on duty when his mother and sisters arrived to visit the Royal Family. The Grand Duke was made Colonel of the regiment in 1984 until his abdication from the throne in 2000. The Duke of Cambridge is the current Colonel.

The 3rd Battalion was disbanded in 1946, and the 2nd the following year. The 1st Battalion was sent to Palestine in 1947; since then it has served in Libya, Germany, Egypt, Cyprus, Aden, Hong Kong (China), Belize, Northern Ireland, Kosovo, Iraq and Afghanistan.

The Irish Guards are unique among regiments of the Household Division in having a living mascot, which parades in front of the battalion: an Irish wolfhound, the ancient hunting dog of Ireland. The first, Brian Boru, was presented to the new regiment in 1902 by the Irish Kennel Club. His serving successor, the 16th in line, is Domhnall.

The motto of the Irish Guards, 'Quis Separabit', is taken from the Epistle of St Paul to the Romans – 'who will separate us'. The original quotation continues 'from the love of God', reminding all Guardsmen of the higher purpose they serve. The motto also speaks of the loyalty they have to their regiments and to each other. It is often used at the funerals of Irish Guardsmen: 'Quis Separabit? Certainly not Death.'

Domhnall, the Irish Guards Irish Wolfhound mascot, is presented to Michael D Higgins, the President of the Irish Republic, during his inspection of a Guard of Honour at Windsor Castle in 2014 on the first ever State Visit to the UK by the country's Head of State. Appropriately enough, 'Domhnall' means 'world leader' in Gaelic.
© MoD Crown Copyright

The Duchess of Cambridge presents shamrock to Domhnall on St Patrick's Day 2014 at Mons Barracks in Aldershot. In 1902 the Irish Wolfhound Club of Northern Ireland offered to provide an Irish Wolfhound as the regimental mascot of the Irish Guards, and the breed has remained the mascot ever since. The ceremony of the presentation of shamrock was inaugurated by Queen Alexandra, wife of Edward VII, in 1901.
© MoD Crown Copyright

The mascot leads the Band of the Irish Guards past the Guards Division Memorial at the beginning of The Queen's Birthday Parade.

THE WELSH GUARDS Shortly after the start of the Great War, on 19 September 1914, the Chancellor of the Exchequer, David Lloyd George, gave an impassioned speech to an audience of London Welshmen: 'I should like to see a Welsh army in the field. I should like to see the race who faced the Normans for hundreds of years in their struggle for freedom, the race that helped to win the Battle of Crécy, the race that fought for a generation against the greatest captain in Europe – I should like to see that race give a good taste of its quality in this struggle. And they are going to do it.'

Before the year was out the 38th (Welsh) Division came into being, and soon after, on 6 February 1915, Field Marshal Lord Kitchener of Khartoum, Secretary of State for War, summoned Major General Sir Francis Lloyd, the General Officer Commanding London District, and ordered him 'to raise a regiment of Welsh Guards'.

The order was obeyed with astonishing speed. The Royal Warrant authorising the raising of the 'Welsh Regiment of Foot Guards to be designated Welsh Guards' – or *Gwarchodlu Cymreig* – was signed by George V 20 days later. Permission was given to Welshmen serving in other Foot Guards regiments to transfer, and 300 came from the Grenadiers alone, joining a further 200 in training at at Caterham, and a full complement of officers.

The first Commanding Officer, William Murray Threipland, himself formerly a Grenadier, commanded the regiment's first King's Guard at Buckingham Palace on St David's Day, 1 March 1915. By 18 March the 1st Battalion was 763 men strong.

A remarkable feature of the Welsh Guards is that so many soldiers share the same surnames. As a result they are differentiated by the last two or three digits of their regimental numbers. The story is told of three new recruits joining the battalion from basic training. Their Company Sergeant Major asked their names. The first replied, 'Jones, Sir.' The Company Sergeant Major asked, 'Don't they teach you anything at the Depot these days? What's your last two?' 'Twenty-four, Sir.' He asked the second his name. 'Davies, Sir.' 'What's your last two?' 'Twenty-two, Sir.' 'And who are you?' he asked the third. 'Radmilovic Eighty-eight, Sir!' came the reply. The only Radmilovic in the Welsh Guards in its 100-year history, he was known as 'Eighty-eight' throughout his service.

On 3 August 1915 the 1st Battalion Welsh Guards was presented with its first Colours; a fortnight later it entrained for France, 1,137 strong; on 25 September it fought its first battle, and won its first Battle Honour, 'Loos'. By the end of the war it had added another 19, and Sergeant Robert Bye had won the regiment's first Victoria Cross in the Third Battle of Ypres.

The 2nd (Reserve) Battalion, formed in August 1915, was merged with the 1st Battalion in 1919. As the threat of war emerged again, it was re-formed in May 1939,

A Welsh Guardsman in Guard Order.

The Prince of Wales, 5th Colonel, Welsh Guards. As Heir Apparent in the Order of Succession, the duty of personifying the British nation will one day be his and he will become Colonel-in-Chief of all seven Household Division regiments. He is also the Senior Colonel of the Household Division and hosts all the Regimental Colonels to dinner at Clarence House on the eve of The Queen's Birthday Parade. At this meeting, under The Prince's guidance, a significant amount of business is done by the Colonels on the evolution of the parade.

and the 3rd Battalion was raised in 1941. The 1st Battalion deployed to France in the British Expeditionary Force. In its first battle, which became its first Battle Honour of the war, 'Defence of Arras', Lieutenant the Honourable Christopher Furness won the regiment's second Victoria Cross, posthumously.

The battalion took part in the fighting withdrawal of the BEF, and embarked for England in the 'miracle of Dunkirk'. An officer from the Warwickshire regiment, one Lloyd Robinson, witnessed their return at Leamington Spa train station when tasked to meet trains carrying survivors and billet them in the town or the nearby camp. His account reveals as much about the Brigade of Guards as do the many more stirring accounts of their gallantry in battle.

He described how bedraggled and battle-weary soldiers and officers would gradually emerge from the carriages, a few still with equipment, but most without rifles or helmets, which had been abandoned in the retreat, and none in organised units. He noticed the end carriage of one train remained shut and he was approached by a Subaltern and an Ensign in the Welsh Guards who asked if this was their final destination. When he replied that it was, the Subaltern told the Sergeant Major to get everyone off the train. Between 40 and 50 men got out, nearly all still with their rifles and helmets, and formed up in two ranks as on parade.

Lloyd Robinson explained that the

The Mannekin Pis *in Brussels dressed in the uniform of a Welsh Guards Regimental Sergeant Major.*
© Brussels Town Hall

men were to be bussed to a camp on the far side of town while the officers were to be billeted in town. The Subaltern replied, 'I don't think you realise that we are Number 3 Company 1st Battalion Welsh Guards and there can be no question of splitting up the officers and men.'

Lloyd Robinson responded that they could all be taken to the camp together by bus. When the Subaltern learned that the camp was about a mile on the other side of Leamington Spa, he said they would rather march – and march they did, very smartly, right through the town and to the camp beyond. The Camp Commandant, a Colonel of the Great War, had been forewarned by Lloyd Robinson of their approach. As they marched in, he turned the guard out to salute them and stood himself at the salute with tears running down his face.

Back in France, the 2nd Battalion had a heroic baptism of fire at Boulogne, with 2nd Battalion Irish Guards holding off the 2nd Panzer Division for three days at a loss of nearly 200 men, killed, wounded and missing. The 3rd Battalion served in North Africa and Italy; between them the three battalions added a further 26 Battle Honours. The Welsh Guards were the first troops to re-enter Brussels on 3 September 1944 after a day-long advance of 100 miles in what was described as 'an armoured dash unequalled for speed in this or any other war', led by Major General Sir Allan Henry Adair. To commemorate the Guards' act of deliverance, every year on this date the city's famous

Mannekin Pis statue is dressed up in a miniature Welsh Guards uniform.

The 3rd Battalion was disbanded in 1946, and the 2nd Battalion placed in suspended animation in 1947. As the British Empire shrank, often it was the 1st Battalion that stayed to the end, serving in Palestine, Suez and Aden, and more recently Northern Ireland, Bosnia, Kosovo, Iraq and Afghanistan. When the Falkland Islands were invaded in 1982 the Welsh Guards formed a significant part of the liberating force despite suffering horrific casualties while still aboard their landing craft. Besides 32 Welsh Guardsmen killed, many sustained burns, the best known being Simon Weston. In Afghanistan losses included one platoon commander, one company commander and battalion commander Lieutenant Colonel Rupert Thorneloe, the first time since the Korean War that a single battalion has lost officers at these three key levels of leadership.

On 9 May 2010, a detachment of 76 Welsh Guardsmen became the first British unit to march through Moscow's Red Square. They joined French, Polish and American soldiers in a parade with Russian troops to mark the 65th anniversary of VE Day.

Everywhere they serve, soldiers of the Welsh Guards carry their motto with pride: 'Cymru am Byth', 'Wales Forever', an ancient battle cry which underlines the loyalty of all Guardsmen to the United Kingdom they serve, and its constituent nations.

The Queen presenting new Colours to the Welsh Guards at Windsor Castle on 30 April 2015.
© MoD Crown Copyright

Opposite: The Massed Bands of the Household Division when percussion is provided both by drums and boots.

THE MASSED BANDS OF THE HOUSEHOLD DIVISION

The bands of the Foot Guards regiments trace their history back to King Charles II's warrant in 1685 authorising the formation of what is now the Band of the Grenadier Guards, which initially comprised 12 hautbois (an early oboe). Their principal duty was to march the Guard from Horse Guards Parade to St James's Palace and play while the sentries were changed, a role not dissimilar to what happens today at the Birthday Parade.

The musicians were hired civilians until 1785 when the Coldstream Guards brought over musicians from Hanover who became attested soldiers. The instrumentation of the three Guards bands was generally two oboes, two clarinets, two bassoons and two horns, with a serpent for the bass line and three flamboyantly dressed black percussionists playing cymbals, tambourine and the jingling johnny. Trumpets and flutes were soon added, with other instruments included as they were invented or older versions improved upon. The major change came with the invention of valves, enabling brass instruments to play a full melody line, while the most recent additions were saxophones in the late 1800s.

Some changes to the drill were required when the Band of the Irish Guards first joined the Massed Bands at the King's Birthday Parade in 1901. The Band of the Welsh Guards was formed during the First World War, so by the time of the 1919 parade in Hyde Park there were five bands from the Brigade of Guards on parade as well as the mounted bands of the Household Cavalry.

The bands have represented the United Kingdom throughout the world with a standard of excellence that reflects on the nation as a whole and forms a major part of its shop window. They were at the forefront of recorded sound from the 1890s, while in 1923 the Band of the Irish Guards became the first military band to broadcast on the BBC. They continued to function during the First World War, playing a vital morale boosting role at home and stirring patriotism to encourage men to enlist. They visited France and Belgium in rotation where their music was greatly appreciated by soldiers during rest periods, including at Talbot House in Poperinge, known as Toc H, and this was commemorated with a march of that title played at the parade in 2015.

One of the slow marches played in 2015 was 'Lord Wellington's March', composed by Princess Charlotte of Wales, the only child of George IV. The Prince of Wales recently discovered this march as a piano score and sent it to the then Senior Director of Music, Lieutenant Colonel Stephen Barnwell, in the hope that he might arrange it for use on the parade to mark the 200th anniversary of Waterloo.

A Sergeant in the Band of the Coldstream Guards.

The musicians' Gold State Coats were ordered by Charles II. When he was unable to pay for the miles of gold thread, the Lord Mayor of London paid instead. In recognition, the Lord Mayor is the only person outside the Royal Family entitled to a Household Cavalry Escort with musicians dressed in State Coats, a debt annually honoured at the Lord Mayor's Show.

The Mounted Band has annual engagements on State occasions, performs in Beating Retreat and plays on a number of Queen's Life Guard mounts. Each regiment has three drum horses – one in the prime of his time, one trained and in use, and one in training. These Shire and Clydesdale horses, with their long manes, tails and feathered feet, can reach 19 hands.

THE GUNS OF THE KING'S TROOP Salutes fired by artillery go back almost as far as their creation. In April 1670 the Duke of Cumberland, as Constable of Windsor Castle, signed an order releasing powder 'for the discharging of Thirteen great guns upon St George's Day'. Today the practice of the firing of Royal Salutes on special days continues in accordance with Queen's Regulations.

The specific dates marked by this honour are: 6 February, The Queen's accession; 21 April, The Queen's birthday; 2 June, the anniversary of the 1953 Coronation; 10 June, The Duke of Edinburgh's birthday; 14 November, The Prince of Wales's birthday. Salutes are also fired for The Queen's Official Birthday, State Visits by Heads of State and the State Opening of Parliament.

A salute of 21 guns is the norm but in Green Park and Hyde Park a further 20 are added to reflect their royal status. At the royal palace of the Tower of London, where the salute is fired by the Honourable Artillery Company, it is 62 guns – the extra 20 are for the City of London.

Although fired elsewhere in Britain it is the London salutes – and those of the King's Troop – which attract the most attention; the impact of the horses and the sudden appearance of six guns at speed are an exciting if short event. The salute for The Queen's Official Birthday and State Visits are always fired in Green Park as the Troop ranks past at Buckingham Palace immediately after firing. These 'trotting salutes' are comparatively sedate but the location in high summer with the oak and plane trees in full leaf is enchanting and more than makes up for the lack of speed. On all other occasions the 'galloping salutes' take part in Hyde Park.

When the King's Troop was stationed at St John's Wood the three sections of two guns were prepared that morning and departure from the Wood did not need to occur until 11:00. Now the Troop is stationed at Woolwich, south of the river, there is a necessity to 'forward base' in Wellington Barracks. In June the Troop has to be forward based for almost two weeks as there can be four salutes in quick succession: Coronation, The Duke of Edinburgh's Birthday, three for The Queen's Birthday Parade and possibly a State Visit too.

Whether it is fired in Green or Hyde Park the salute is a genuine spectacle for the public. It is an opportunity for the King's Troop to demonstrate its fine equestrian skills and professionalism and for spectators to imagine the thrill and adrenalin of a battery of yesteryear's guns coming into action for real.

41-Round Royal Gun
Salute in Green Park.

The Sovereign's Standard of The Life Guards.

THE STANDARDS Standards in the Household Cavalry have a very similar role and symbolism to Colours in a Foot Guard battalion but there are important differences. Whereas the Colours in an infantry battalion marked the centre of the line and were an important rallying point in battle, cavalry regiments found that charging with theirs could be inconvenient, and, although the Standards have always been an important way of representing the regiments' loyalty and service, they would sometimes be lodged behind the lines for safe keeping.

Any parade, whether daily Queen's Life Guard when Her Majesty is in residence or a Sovereign's Escort on a State occasion, a Standard will be carried on parade. In contrast with the Foot Guards, where the Colour is carried by a junior officer, the Household Cavalry Standards are carried by a Squadron Corporal Major or Staff Corporal. For The Queen's Birthday Parade, the Sovereign's Standard of The Life Guards and of The Blues and Royals alternate annually, with the colour of the Standard dictating the appointments and formation of the Household Cavalry on parade.

The regiment forms up on the square for the Commanding Officer's Inspection. Once the other ranks have been inspected, the officers are inspected on the approach ramp, before the officers and field officers join the regiment on the square. Once formed up, the Field Officer will order the regiment to draw swords. This is combined with a Royal Salute, given as the Squadron Corporal Major rides forward to receive the Standard. As the Corporal Major cannot draw his sword while carrying the Standard, he is escorted at all times by soldiers with drawn swords. The Standard is marched onto the square, again with an escort, by soldiers from the Headquarters Squadron. The Squadron Corporal Major then takes up his place in the centre of the parade.

The Blues and Royals uniquely hold a Guidon as well as Sovereign's and Union Standards, as a result of the 1969 amalgamation of The Royal Horse Guards (Blues) and the 1st Royal Dragoons (Royals). At the centre of its distinctive dovetailed rectangular shape is the Royal Cypher surrounded by a wreath of the English rose, the Scottish thistle and the Irish shamrock. The corners retain the royal crest of England, the white horse of Hanover for George I and the 105th Imperial Eagle captured at Waterloo. Unlike The Blues and Royals' Standards, the Guidon has non-identical sides displaying a total of 47 different Battle Honours on both sides. The first dates to 1680, the Battle of Tangier, which is the earliest Battle Honour awarded to the British Army. The most recent is Iraq, 2003. The Guidon is generally used when The Queen's Standard is on an Escort and a Turnout is required by a Blues and Royals Queen's Life Guard. A new Guidon is received only every 30 years; the next presentation is in 2035.

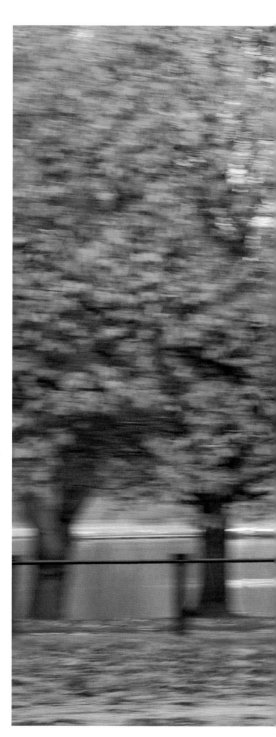

The Regimental Corporal Major carrying the Sovereign's Standard of The Blues and Royals.

*The Guidon of
The Blues and Royals.*

T HE COLOURS Warriors have used different means for identifying themselves, sending messages and as rallying points in battle, for as long as war has been waged. These methods range from uniform clothing and badges to distinguish groups and individuals, to field signs, including flags, used by commanders to indicate their location to their followers.

From the early Middle Ages these latter were known as Standards, and were first recorded in descriptions of the Battle of the Standard in 1138. In this battle, the English repelled an invading Scottish army near Northallerton. The English commander, William, Earl of Aumale, set up a ship's mast on a cart, decked with banners from local monasteries, to mark the centre of his battle line. Richard, Prior of Hexham, wrote a contemporary account of the sight: 'On the top of this pole they hung a silver pyx containing the Host, and the banner of St Peter the Apostle, and John of Beverley and Wilfrid of Ripon, confessors and bishops. In doing this, their hope was that our Lord Jesus Christ, by the efficacy of his Body, might be their leader in the contest in which they were engaging in defence of his church and their country. By this means they also provided for their men, that, in the event of their being cut off and separated from them, they might observe some certain and conspicuous rallying-point, by which they might rejoin their comrades, and where they would receive succour.'

By this time it was normal for each knight to have his own sign in the form of a banner on his lance depicting his heraldic coat of arms; several are shown in the Bayeux Tapestry. Knights' flags became generally known as their Standards.

By the end of the Middle Ages not every military commander had his own coat of arms; in the 16th century in the time of Queen Elizabeth I, it is recorded that many 'low born captains in the infantry' had plain coloured flags to distinguish them and their companies. These flags became known as Colours; until 1707, every company in the British Army carried such a Colour, emblazoned with its commander's insignia. By then the battalion, composed of several (typically ten) companies, had become the normal tactical unit in the infantry. The three senior officers, the 'field' officers (a Colonel, Lieutenant Colonel and Major in each battalion), commanded the battalion's three wings (centre, left and right flanks) in battle. They doubled as the Captains of the three senior companies.

In 1707 the number of Colours in British line infantry battalions was reduced to these three, one plain, with the regiment's or its Colonel's crest, and two Union Flags. In the Foot Guards, Captains' Colours continued to be issued to each company until 1838. In 1747 it was ordained that each battalion should have only two Colours: the King's Colour (the Union Flag) and the Regimental Colour. The Foot Guards,

The Second Queen's Colour of the 1st Battalion Grenadier Guards carried by the Nijmegen Company.

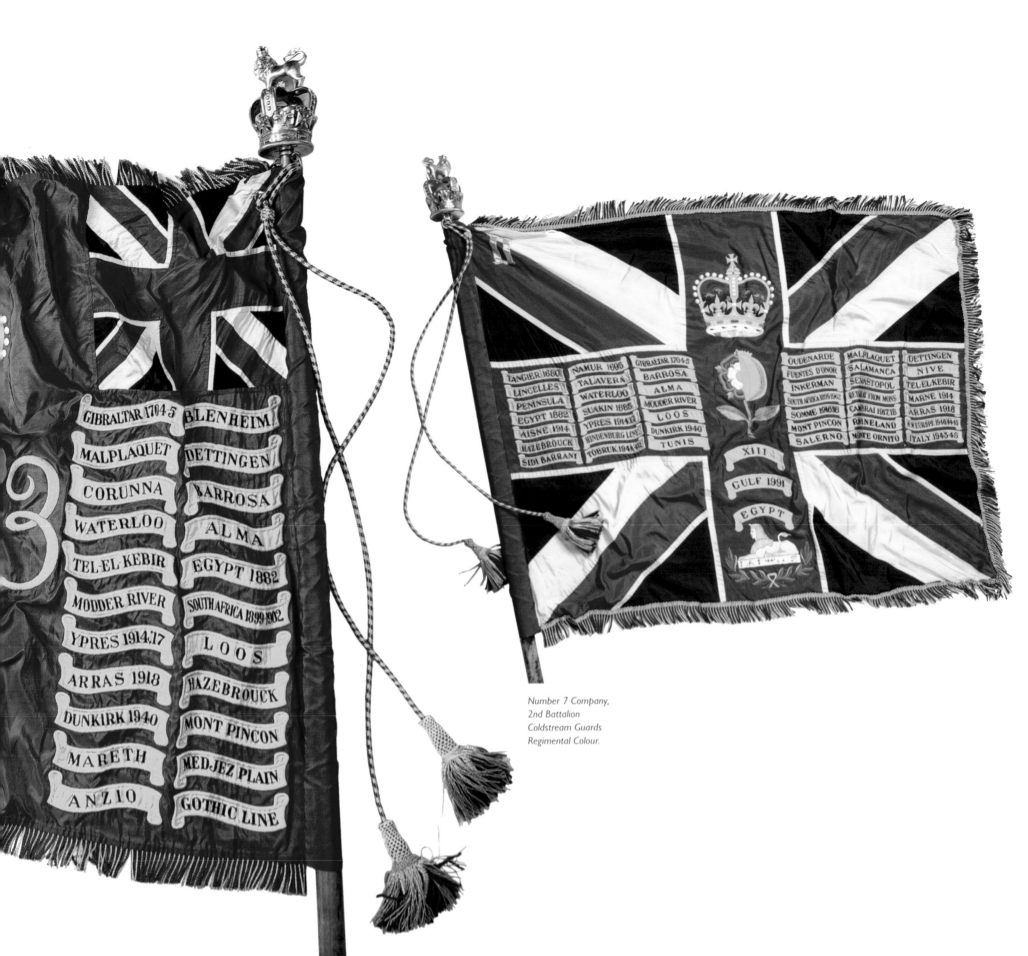

GIBRALTAR 1704·5 BLENHEIM

MALPLAQUET DETTINGEN

CORUNNA BARROSA

WATERLOO ALMA

TEL·EL·KEBIR EGYPT 1882

MODDER RIVER SOUTH AFRICA 1899·1902

YPRES 1914·17 LOOS

ARRAS 1918 HAZEBROUCK

DUNKIRK 1940 MONT PINCON

MARETH MEDJEZ PLAIN

ANZIO GOTHIC LINE

TANGIER 1680 NAMUR 1695 GIBRALTAR 1704·5 OUDENARDE MALPLAQUET DETTINGEN
LINCELLES TALAVERA BARROSA FUENTES D'ONOR SALAMANCA NIVE
PENINSULA WATERLOO ALMA INKERMAN SEVASTOPOL TEL·EL·KEBIR
EGYPT 1882 SUAKIN 1885 MODDER RIVER SOUTH AFRICA 1899·1902 RETREAT FROM MONS MARNE 1914
AISNE 1914 YPRES 1914·17 LOOS SOMME 1916·18 CAMBRAI 1917,18 ARRAS 1918
HAZEBROUCK HINDENBURG LINE DUNKIRK 1940 MONT PINCON RHINELAND N.W.EUROPE 1940.44·45
SIDI BARRANI TOBRUK 1941·42 TUNIS SALERNO MONTE ORNITO ITALY 1943·45

XIII

GULF 1991

EGYPT

Number 7 Company,
2nd Battalion
Coldstream Guards
Regimental Colour.

however, stuck to the old tradition, that the King's Colour had the regimental crest or badge, and the Regimental Colour was the Union Flag. It became the practice to emblazon the Colours with Honorary Distinctions, commonly known as Battle Honours.

The Grenadier, Coldstream and Scots Guards have all been honoured by the Sovereign at different times in their history with the award of other Colours. Since its foundation, the senior company of the Grenadier Guards, The Queen's Company, has carried a special Company Colour, which is also the Royal Standard of the regiment. Larger than The Queen's and Regimental Colours, it is only carried when The Queen is present, and only ever lowered to her. The Coldstream Guards have two State Colours of similar sizes, and the Scots Guards have one, which are also only carried in the presence of the Sovereign.

Throughout the 18th century and much of the 19th, Standards and Colours continued to be carried in battle. The last recorded instance of a British regiment carrying their Colours into action was the 58th (Rutlandshire) Regiment of Foot (later the Northamptonshire Regiment) when it fought the Boers on 28 January 1881 in the Battle of Laing's Nek.

Long before this point Colours had acquired unique significance to their regiments. They had come to embody the history, traditions and spirit of the regiment to which they belonged. Such was their potency that men would fight

to the last man standing to protect them in battle, and their capture by the enemy brought shame upon the regiment.

Blessed and consecrated when they are presented, the Colours also bring a sacramental quality to every parade in which they are carried; they are usually laid up, when replaced, in churches dear to the regiment in question. At all times they are handled with reverence; parading them through the ranks, 'Trooping the Colour', is therefore much more than an arcane ceremony. It is the restatement of the loyalty, courage and sacrifice of the regiment and its members throughout their history.

The Queen's Company Colour is the Royal Standard of the Grenadier Guards and was presented by Her Majesty as Colonel of the regiment on 14 April 1953. The St Edward's Crown features centrally and above the badges of the rose of England, the Scottish thistle and the Irish shamrock in each corner. The Queen's Company, in recognition of its senior status in the regiment, has the privilege of carrying the Colour when it is taken out by the 1st Battalion. The Queen's, or Sovereign's, Company plays a particularly special role at the beginning and end of the Sovereign's reign: it has the honour of being on duty in Westminster Abbey on the occasion of the coronation; it performs the solemn duty of watching over the dead body of a Sovereign prior to any public lying-in-state; and it provides the Bearer Party at the Sovereign's funeral. The Company Colour is buried with the Sovereign at the Committal.

Two Ensigns each with a Colour changing over the Guard at Buckingham Palace. They march around the forecourt 'pacing the minutes'.
© MoD Crown Copyright

Foot Guards Colours in the Guards Chapel, the earliest of which date from 1770. When the Foot Guards battalions returned from the Crimea they applied for new Colours and on 27 February 1857 the Colours from the battlefields of the Alma and Inkerman were deposited in the Guards Chapel. It had been customary for retired Colours to be the perquisite of the Colonel, and many had been dispersed across the land. In response to an appeal for their return for display in their spiritual home, the Guards Chapel, many found their way back.

HOBSON & SONS LTD

One of the aspects of British ceremonial which Britons take for granted but foreigners never do is authenticity. In purpose, movement, dress and the symbols used, quality is always to the fore. Nowhere is quality more evident than in the Colours and Standards of the Household Division. Originating through time and carried daily on duty, each symbolises the undying attachment of the five regiments of Foot Guards and two regiments of Cavalry sworn to protect the Sovereign at all times.

Today's Colours and Standards would be recognisable to Guardsmen and Troopers of every era, although the initials of the reigning Sovereign change as do the Battle Honours. If there is to be a 'new' design it originates from the College of Arms under the expert watch of the Inspector of Arms and the Deputy Inspector, who ensure that the design which is presented to The Queen for her approval is at the apogee of heraldic art and craft.

Should The Queen approve the paintings, she signs them, and photographs of the highest quality are made for the chosen production house, which in the case of the Household Division is Hobson & Sons Ltd. Established in 1850 in Woolwich, close to the Royal Artillery Barracks, by Mrs Hobson, a redoubtable seamstress with a head for business, the firm quickly became known for the quality of its work. In just a decade it expanded to five shops, fit employment for Mrs Hobson's growing family. With the burgeoning of the Empire, in the 1880s a site in Soho's Lexington Street was acquired where gold and silver wire embroidery was produced and lace woven. In the basement, the Leather Accoutrements department produced specialist goods of all descriptions. Hobson's later expanded to Tooley Street, between London and Tower Bridges, where several hundred highly skilled artisans, many of Huguenot descent, manufactured everything

Emma Gilbert finishing the hem and fringe on The Queen's Colour of the Welsh Guards.

The shields are being sewn by Susan Jones who has been making the Colours for over 30 years. She is the principal embroiderer and makes four Colours a year.

needed for dressing the Army, including its horses, from head to toe.

In the 1930s Hobson's bought a disused church hall with a plot of surrounding land at Thundersley, Essex to enable it to bring all the parts of its business together under one roof, an aim not finally achieved until the 1990s. During the Second World War the Thundersley site manufactured large numbers of tropical uniforms, and after the war new export markets grew as countries achieved independence.

Today Hobson's occupies over 30,000 square feet in its Essex base, where generations of the same families ply age-old accomplishments largely lost in this modern world creating products that are exported to more than 80 nations. In addition to uniforms, an extraordinary array of accoutrements and accessories is offered in its catalogue. Stable belts, buckles and sword slings; uniform sashes, epaulettes, lanyards, aiguilettes and other plaited items; webbing, holsters and anklets; leather belts, crossbelts and Sam Brownes; gauntlets, gloves, boots and shoes; plumes, spurs and whistles; pace sticks, batons, canes, swords and scabbards; embroidered, metallic and enamelled badges.

One of the most visible items on parade are the chinstraps of all the regiments' headdress, made by Steve Barwell who has worked for Hobson's for 35 years.

It is the Standards and Colours it produces, however, for which Hobson's is most renowned. The firm's highly trained embroiderers will spend some 600 to 900 hours of painstaking needlework on the heaviest red silk available: the raised letters, the spelling of battles, the piping and foliage, gold, silver embroidery, the bold contrasting primary colours set out in the certified painting, all stitched with care and precision until every element comes alive on the embroiderer's bench.

To begin with, a single piece of silk is marked on one side and then fixed within a wooden frame under tension. The embroiderer then lines up the right weight of threads dyed to the shades specified by the Ministry of Defence and in-house working guides. The majority of the embroidery is through a single piece of silk with both sides being produced at the same time to the same quality. This demands the highest level of skill. Where text is present within the centres and Battle Honours these are embroidered separately and appliquéd onto the Colour or Standard on both sides. When the embroiderers have finished, the art work (for such it is) is removed from the frame and passed to the hand finishers who trim it to the correct measurements before applying the fringe and pocket lining.

Then, following a close inspection by Richard Withnall, Hobson's head of production, along with Ministry of Defence and regimental representatives, the nod is given and the Colour or Standard leaves Thundersley under police escort. At the end of its journey it is reverentially taken into the regimental vaults in Wellington or Hyde Park Barracks until they are presented to The Queen, blessed and brought into service. The retiring Colours or Standards they replace are eventually put on public display at various appropriate sites around the country or at the Royal Military Chapel (the Guards' Chapel).

The Welsh Dragon at the centre of the Welsh Guards' Queen's Colour.

BATTLE HONOURS During the 18th century it became customary to emblazon the Colours or Standards of a regiment with its Honorary Distinctions, more commonly known as its Battle Honours. Most regiments in the British Army have earned so many that not all of them can fit on their Colours; those that do appear on them are retained by virtue of their particular hard-won significance. Hence the Grenadiers only carry 45 of their 74 Battle Honours on their Colours, and date the adoption of the custom to 1812. The Scots Guards Colours bear a similar number of their 89, as do the Coldstream Guards of their extraordinary total of 117.

Most are written in words, often with their date: 'Tangier 1680' or 'Gulf 1991'; a few have special emblems, like the Sphinx, for the campaign against Napoleon in Egypt. The Colours are decked with laurel wreaths on the anniversaries of the battles they commemorate.

The Standard of The Blues and Royals.

The Regimental Colours of Nijmegen Company, 2nd Battalion Grenadier Guards.

FOOT GUARDS

The Battle Honours of the Foot Guards are not restricted to their Colours, but can be found in much of the regimental regalia and equipment. For example, they are emblazoned in 22 carat gold paint on the various regimental drums, and embroidered on Drum Majors' baldrics. They are also inscribed around the ring on the dome of the Drum Major's staff, and if there is insufficient room on the ring, Battle Honours scrolls are affixed to the dome of the staff too.

Special honours are commemorated in other ways as well. Victory over the French Imperial Guard at Waterloo is commemorated by the bearskin caps worn by the Foot Guards. Close inspection of the lace which decorates the tunics of Foot Guards drummers reveals that it is embroidered with royal blue fleurs de lys: an echo of the claim of the Kings of England to the throne of France.

In common with all other ranks in the Foot Guards, their boots have 13 studs in the soles, one for each Victoria Cross won by Guardsmen in the Crimean War. Guardsmen's blue-grey greatcoats are also said to have been taken from the Russians in the same war.

A much more recent commemoration is that of the liberation of Brussels on 3 September 1944 by the Guards Armoured Division; for their part in it the Welsh Guards have the honour of dressing the statue of the *Mannequin Pis* in their uniform on the anniversary.

The baldric of the Senior Drum Major, Household Division, with the badge of the Division bearing its motto, 'Septem Juncta in Uno' ('Seven Joined in One'), above the badges of each of the regiments.

The Drum Major's baldric.

1st Battalion Scots Guards drum.

Waterloo Battle Honour on a Coldstream Guards officer's sword. The interlocking triangle design on the Wilkinson sword is an ancient symbol denoting unbreakable strength.

Battle Honours engraved on the hilts of Grenadier swords.

HOUSEHOLD CAVALRY

The Battle Honours of The Life Guards and
The Blues and Royals are proudly displayed on
the shabraques, the embroidered cloths worn
under the saddles of both the officers and the
regimental drum horses. Both regiments have
so many Battle Honours that they cannot all
be shown so a selection is made, particularly
of the many battles in the First and Second
World Wars.

On these drum horse shabraques the great
honours of the Peninsula and Waterloo are
displayed alongside honours from the Boer
War; note that Iraq appears for both 1941
and 2003. Souleuvre refers to one of the most
celebrated incidents in the Second World War,
when, during the breakout from Normandy,
the 2nd Household Cavalry Regiment found
an unguarded bridge over that river which the
Allies exploited, leading to their subsequent
victory at Falaise. Other recent Battle
Honours include the Gulf in 1991 for The Life
Guards and the Falklands in 1982 for The Blues
and Royals.

It is of note how many Battle Honours refer to
wars in the same countries over the centuries:
not just Iraq and North Africa but also France,
the Low Countries and Germany.

*Dismounted Review
Order belt buckle.*

*The Life Guards
shabraque on the left
and The Blues and
Royals on the right.*

Corporal Major's Standard belt.

The cartouche box of a Life Guards officer. Traditionally worn under the arm to carry messages or ammunition, suspended from a crossbelt that once doubled as a spare girth, it is now strapped tightly to the centre of the back.

THE WATERLOO MEDAL

The Waterloo medal was the first medal issued by the British Government to all soldiers who had fought in a battle, regardless of rank. Commissioned shortly after the battle by Sir William Wellesley Pole, brother of the Duke of Wellington, it features an image of the Prince Regent, and on the reverse, a seated figure of Victory. The medal was initially commissioned in bronze but was changed to silver by the Prince Regent, flouting the convention that medals reflected army hierarchy. Medals for Generals and senior officers were made of gold, while silver-gilt was used for field officers and general staff, silver for Captains and Subalterns, bronze for native commissioned and European non-commissioned officers, and tin for privates. Wellington wanted all soldiers of all ranks who fought at Waterloo to receive the same medal in recognition of the equal part they played in the campaign and his gratitude for their bravery.

THE ROYALS' CAPTURE OF THE EAGLE AT WATERLOO

Eagles were as important to Napoleon's infantry regiments as their Colours were to a British infantry battalion. Eagles were part of Napoleonic symbolism, presented personally by the Emperor, who would also investigate any loss. Made of silver or gold and carried atop a long pole, they were decorated with streamers listing the regimental Battle Honours. Removed, understandably, by the Bourbons on their restoration in 1814, they were re-presented with great ceremony by Napoleon on the Champ de Mars soon after his restoration.

At Waterloo the 105th Ligne was the lead regiment in General Donzelot's division, and moved off to attack the allied positions as part of D'Erlon's Corps; this was to be Napoleon's main effort, the blow with which he expected to shatter Wellington's thinly held line. Taking terrible casualties from British artillery, the 105th nevertheless breasted the allies' ridge line, routed a Dutch infantry brigade, and withstood a determined attack by General Picton's infantry battalions.

It looked as if Napoleon's plan may have succeeded when Lord Uxbridge ordered the British Heavy Cavalry Brigades to charge. The left-hand squadron of The Royals crashed directly into the 105th, with Captain Alexander Clark and Corporal F Stiles capturing the Eagle. Clark cut down the man carrying it, and, having failed to break the pole so that he could secrete it under his jacket, claims he told Stiles to carry it to the rear. After the battle there was a bitter controversy in the regiment as to who exactly did capture it, but Clark was promoted and decorated while Stiles was commissioned. The Eagle is today in the National Army Museum, and the symbolic bird and the number 105 form part of The Blues and Royals crest, worn on the left shoulder.

THE GUNS AT WATERLOO

The actions of the Royal Horse Artillery at Waterloo are justly revered. Eight of its 15 Troops fought on 18 June 1815, and Wellington used their exceptional manoeuvrability to devastating effect.

The opposing commanders deployed their artillery very differently. Napoleon, a gunner himself, massed his in a grand battery of 84 guns, which opened the battle with a great cannonade. The guns had limited success because of Wellington's tactic of deploying most of his army out of sight on the reverse slopes of his position. The British artillery was used much more flexibly. The field artillery batteries closely supported the infantry, breaking up the massed French attacks, with the gunners taking cover in the infantry squares at the last moment. When possible they took the wheels of their guns with them, to prevent the French towing them away. The eight RHA Troops, with six guns each, were divided for a variety of tasks. Two supported the cavalry brigades; of the remaining six, four were up-gunned with 9-pounders, and one, most unusually, with 5 1/2 inch howitzers, much heavier than most horse artillery. This Troop was deployed first to strengthen the allied centre, then at noon to the right flank, as massive French attacks threatened the Foot Guards defending Hougoumont. In the afternoon it was switched again, moving forward to help break up the massed cavalry assaults in the centre.

One of the other Troops, protecting the left flank, was redeployed to the centre at the culmination of the battle, to help retake La Haye Sainte, the farmhouse in front of the allied centre.

Wellington, never given to hyperbole, warmly praised how the Royal Horse Artillery 'advanced with an alacrity and rapidity most admirable; that is how I like to see horse artillery move'.

THE FOOT GUARDS AT WATERLOO

The Foot Guards had special status from their inception, sharing with the Household Cavalry the privilege of guarding the Sovereign. This meant that they were usually stationed in or near London, which enhanced their social appeal: in the days of purchasing commissions, those in the Household Troops were the most expensive of all.

This led to some teasing by the rest of the Army; in the Napoleonic Wars they were often referred to as 'Hyde Park soldiers' or the 'gentlemen's sons'. With their own chain of command based in Horse Guards, and reporting straight to the palace, their deployments were jealously guarded by the Sovereign: royal assent was required to send them overseas.

Despite the teasing, their appearance in a campaign was always welcomed for they were always well recruited and trained. It was owing to their quality that Wellington chose the Foot Guards to defend Hougoumont, the critical outpost on the right of his line at Waterloo, just as he chose the King's German Legion to defend La Haye Sainte in the centre.

When Napoleon threw in his invincible Imperial Guard in a final attempt to break the allies, Wellington personally commanded the 1st Guards Brigade to deliver the withering fire that defeated 'the Immortals'.

Some remembered his order as 'Up, Guards, and at 'em'; others recalled a more prosaic 'Now is your time'; but whatever the wording, it was the culminating moment in the battle that ended the Napoleonic Wars, and gave Europe peace for an unprecedented 50 years.

Certainly there is no greater victory in the history of the British Army, or the regiments of the Household Division.

THE BRAVEST MAN

In Wellington's own words, 'the success of the battle turned on the closing of the gates at Hougoumont'. The names of Lieutenant Colonel James Macdonell and Corporal James Graham, both of the Coldstream Guards, are most closely linked to this heroic action.

While fierce hand-to-hand fighting was still taking place inside Hougoumont, more French soldiers were trying to force entry through the Great Gate. Macdonell gathered a group of nine other men, five Coldstreamers and four from the 3rd Guards, who fought their way to the gate. Macdonell and Graham, both well-built men, put their shoulders to the gate, while the others added their weight or thrust back the enemy. As the panels slowly came together, men rushed to gather timbers to reinforce the gate until the great crossbar could fall into place.

Corporal Graham was immediately promoted to Sergeant, and awarded an annual annuity by Reverend John Norcross of Framlingham, but the annuity ceased two years later when the rector went bankrupt. In his will, however, he left £500 for 'the bravest man in England'. Asked to nominate the recipient, Wellington named Macdonell, but the Colonel gallantly shared the award with Sergeant Graham.

'After the Closing of the Gates', by Ernest Crofts, hangs in the Cavalry and Guards Club.

THE HOUSEHOLD CAVALRY STANDARDS PARADE

Every ten years The Queen presents new Standards to the Household Cavalry on Horse Guards Parade, reinforcing the 350-year bond of service between The Life Guards and The Blues and Royals, and their Sovereign. The last ceremony was in May 2014, when two squadrons from the Household Cavalry Regiment in Windsor, crewing their light armoured vehicles with which they are equipped for their reconnaissance role, joined four Mounted Divisions, two of Life Guards and two of The Blues and Royals, from the Household Cavalry Mounted Regiment, based at Hyde Park Barracks.

Both The Life Guards and The Blues and Royals have a Sovereign's Standard and three Squadron Standards, originally the Standards carried by the individual troops. They are all of dark crimson, emblazoned with the regiments' Battle Honours, and carried in a stirrup bucket by a Warrant Officer or senior Staff Corporal as opposed to an officer. This can be quite tricky as not all horses take kindly to a large flag flapping around behind their ears, and in each regiment the larger and more placid horses tend to be reserved as 'Standard Horses'. The Standards are in regular use. One is carried behind Her Majesty on State occasions and also on The Queen's Life Guard when the Court is in residence in London. 2014's Standards Parade began with the arrival of the Band of The Blues and Royals, followed by the squadrons' vehicles, the roar of their diesel engines and the grinding of their tracks causing some surprise to Londoners more used to the gentler sounds of marching and military music. These CVR(T) vehicles, as they are known, have been in service since 1974 when they were first used in the Cyprus emergency. Originally designed for use in the plantations of Malaya, they weigh just over 10 tons and were narrow enough to fit between the rows of rubber trees. They have been used in almost every operation since, from the

The Queen presenting new Standards to the Household Cavalry on Horse Guards Parade, accompanied by the Major General, now Silver Stick, and watched by both Gold Sticks.
© MoD Crown Copyright

Lieutenant Colonel Sir Andrew Ford, Comptroller, Lord Chamberlain's Office, the Major General and Palace staff rehearsing the presentation of new Standards. The officers are wearing the traditional plain clothes worn in London: hard felt (or coke) hats, stiff collars and carrying furled umbrellas.

Falklands to Afghanistan. Next to appear was the Band of The Life Guards, leading in the Mounted Squadrons of the Household Cavalry Mounted Regiment with the two Commanding Officers. The two bands were amalgamated in 2014 to form the Band of the Household Cavalry, the only mounted band in the British Army.

The old Standards, which had been spruced up for their last parade by the skilled regimental tailors, were received with a Royal Salute, the same honour as the regiments present to The Queen. The two Colonels – the Princess Royal, Colonel of The Blues and Royals, and Field Marshal the Lord Guthrie of Craigiebank, Colonel of The Life Guards – were conducted to the dais and also received with a Royal Salute. They watched the old Standards being trooped and leaving the parade ground.

The regiments' magnificent solid silver kettledrums, presented to The Blues by George III in 1805 and to The Life Guards by William IV in 1831, were brought to the centre of the parade and the eight new Standards – four for each regiment – were placed upon them in readiness for the Service of Consecration.

The Queen arrived from Buckingham Palace in the company of the Travelling Escort carrying the Sovereign's Standard. She was received by the Colonels and the Major General Commanding the Household Division and was conducted onto the dais for the Royal Salute and the playing of the National Anthem.

The first rehearsal before dawn.

The second rehearsal with practice standards.

The Queen was then led to the centre of the parade ground by the two Colonels, and followed by the clergy who performed the consecration. The Queen then presented the new Standards to the Commanding Officers who then handed them to the Mounted Standard Bearers.

In her address The Queen noted that the Household Cavalry, 'in its Armoured Reconnaissance role, has been at the very forefront of operations, and especially so in Iraq and Afghanistan'.

The regiment has had nine tours in these countries since 2004, making it one of the most frequently deployed units in the British Army, while suffering 15 fatalities and many serious injuries in the line of duty.

The Queen paid tribute to the soldiers' families who shared the 'burdens' of this 'time of sacrifice and separation'. These families joined their serving relatives at a Garden Party at Buckingham Palace later in the afternoon to celebrate the regiment's special day.

During the March Past of the Mounted and Armoured Squadrons the spectators stood in respect as the Standards passed them. The new Standards were immediately pressed into service the following day for the daily Guard Change, and for their first Royal Escort, made up of four mounted divisions of over 100 men, for the State Opening of Parliament the following week.

Top left: The old Standards being ranked off to 'Auld Lang Syne'.

Top right: The new Standards being marched on.

Middle left: The Standards being blessed.

Middle right: The Commanding Officer handing the new Standard to a Corporal Major.

Bottom left: The drums about to be cased and marched off.

Bottom right: The new Standards being ranked past The Queen.

THE MAJOR GENERAL'S INSPECTION OF THE HOUSEHOLD CAVALRY MOUNTED REGIMENT During the winter, once the last State Visit has been concluded, as many horses as can be spared from The Queen's Life Guard have a winter break at the Defence Animal Centre in Melton Mowbray, where they are turned out to grass. They return wild and woolly, with shaggy winter coats and covered in mud. During this time, new soldiers will have come through the riding course and new horses (known as 'remounts') will be completing their training. Thus a series of inspections is begun to ensure readiness for the start of the State Ceremonial season.

The squadrons embark on a prolonged programme of clipping and grooming, with the farriers working flat out, to be ready for the Commanding Officer's Horse Inspection, at which every horse is trotted up and condition is assessed. The saddlers will be working hard to refit saddles as horses regain the muscle lost on their holiday: every piece of tack is shaped to the horse, and stamped with that horse's name. Equally, every man's state uniform is also inspected, with the tailors carrying out tasks from trimming plumes to the correct length to refitting tunics, while the saddlers make any adjustment to the leather parts of the uniform as required. Much cleaning must be done. The Riding Staff lead a programme of fitness training for the horses, and men and horses progress from riding in the school and on the roads, to practising manoeuvres as troops, squadrons and finally as a regiment.

This whole process is then validated by a series of inspections by the Riding Master, the Adjutant, the Commanding Officer, and finally the Major General Commanding the Household Division. This comprises a springtime parade in Hyde Park that replicates much of The Queen's Birthday Parade, with the full mounted bands (now amalgamated as the Band of the Household Cavalry) on parade as well. The regiment carries out a walk past, a trot past and a canter past, before performing an Advance in Review Order – a very orderly cavalry charge.

The inspection then continues in the barracks, with every troop being inspected for its procedures, its care of horses, men and equipment. Troop Leaders are quizzed by the Brigade Major to ensure that they know a 'Form Sections' from a 'Reform the Division', and even the padre and doctor are required to ride.

As the parade is on grass, giving the horses a dangerous sense of freedom, with all the yapping dogs and fluttering plastic bags that a park brings, the early rehearsals can be a major test of inexperienced soldiers and horses. The remounts are all ridden by members of the Riding Staff, marked out by a badge depicting a spur on the right arm, but even they can struggle to contain an overexcited half-ton youngster with one hand. After this, the rest of the ceremonial season should be simple by comparison!

The Major General saluting the Standard of The Blues and Royals during his inspection.

One of the few occasions when these headdresses are all on parade together. The Medical Officer wears a black plumed hat. To his left is the Nurse from the Royal Army Medical Corps. The Veterinary Officer wears a red plumed hat. The Padre wears a black cocked hat and the Admin Officer is in Blues.

The Commanding Officer Lieutenant Colonel Paul Bedford 'cutting'.

THE MAJOR GENERAL'S REVIEW OF THE KING'S TROOP A key date in the calendar of the King's Troop is its spring inspection by the General Officer Commanding Household and London District. Under his scrutiny 54 riders in full ceremonial dress, 72 immaculately groomed horses and six gleaming guns are put through their paces in Regent's Park, hoping to be declared 'fit to represent the nation' in the busy State Ceremonial and Public Duties season ahead.

The inspection begins at Wellington Barracks, where the General Officer rides among the Troop, inspecting the standard of kit, the soldiers, the officers and the guns. The men and women of the Troop have spent several days polishing leather and brass, and behind every groomed mane, perfectly trimmed tail and glinting spur lie hours of physical effort, dedication and early mornings.

Then the inspection moves to the royal park where the Troop performs its renowned Musical Drive, one of the world's most spectacular displays of horsemanship. Its complex choreographed manoeuvres are laden with risk and must be executed with precision timing. No mean feat when the teams of six colour-matched horses are each drawing six 13-pounder guns.

Many of the moves of the Musical Drive, which is rehearsed twice a week and performed annually at the Royal Windsor Horse Show, have remained unchanged since the late 19th century. In a brochure for the Royal Tournament of 1932, held at Olympia, the spectacle was described thus: 'After performing various simple turns, inclines and circles, one half battery changes rein, and the "Scissors" is carried out. The two half batteries then form up at the ends of the arena, the "Charge" is sounded, and the teams gallop through each other, wheel round the ends of the arena by half batteries and then wheel into line at close interval.'

Each 13-pounder gun and limber weighs 1.5 tons, has no brakes and, when combined with the team of six horses, is approximately 54 feet long. The 13-pounder horse artillery gun was introduced in 1904, after the South African War of 1899–1902 had highlighted the British Army's need to modernise its weaponry, and was used throughout the First World War.

Musicians from the Band of the Royal Artillery accompany the manoeuvres, managing to be heard above the clanking and jangling of the harness and limbers, and the rhythmic pounding of 288 hooves. Depending on the recent weather conditions, the grass either raises clouds of dust or clods of mud under the impact of the horses and the saluting guns. By the end of the inspection, the King's Troop will have ensured their capability, and will return to barracks to remove the dust, mud and grass and prepare for their next duties of the season.

Colonel Hugh Bodington, Chief of Staff, Headquarters London District, inspecting elements of the King's Troop during the Major General's Review.

THE MAJOR GENERAL'S REVIEW OF THE GRENADIER GUARDS

THE MAJOR GENERAL'S REVIEW OF THE GRENADIER GUARDS The Major General's Inspection is one of the most important events in the annual calendar of a Foot Guards battalion. In the recent past, each battalion was inspected every year, but today's high tempo of operations means that his visits are not always inspections, though they are taken very seriously, as the focus for demonstrating and maintaining the unique standards and ethos of the Household Division. Formal inspections are now generally reserved for those trooping their Colour, or returning from a tour away from Public Duties. The inspection looks at every part of a battalion and every aspect of its operation, with a special focus on drill and turnout. It thus fulfils a similar function to the Major General's Reviews of the King's Troop and the Household Cavalry, as a vital part of preparations for The Queen's Birthday Parade and the ceremonial season.

The inspection follows a well-tried sequence in order to confirm the standards of a Foot Guards battalion across the spectrum of routine activity: administration, training, education, equipment and drill. All are examined minutely, usually starting with a formal inspection of the battalion on parade in its smartest uniforms. For those on Public Duties, in London or Windsor, this means tunics. The Major General inspects each man personally, accompanied by key members of the Household Division staff: the Brigade Major, the Garrison Sergeant Major and the Regimental Tailor, checking each uniform and marking it for adjustment. The Regimental Band, Corps of Drums and, for the Scots and Irish Guards, the Pipe Band are generally inspected first, so that they can play for the rest of the inspection. Headquarters Company comes next, so that the battalion's administrators and logisticians can fall out and be inspected by the staff experts in every aspect of their technical responsibilities for supporting the battalion.

It is then the turn of the rifle companies and specialist platoons, the bulk of the battalion.

One by one the various companies are dismissed to change into 'second orders': the second, afternoon phase of the inspection, when each sub-unit is inspected in different orders of dress. A further hurdle is the ritual examination of the junior officers' Regimental Knowledge, in the Orderly Room (the office shared by the Commanding Officer and the Adjutant), by the Brigade Major.

Inspections do not always go perfectly; very occasionally the dread words 'Show Again!' issue forth from the Inspecting Officer, and the whole or part of the process is repeated.

It is to be hoped, however, that finally another Major General's inspection will draw to a successful conclusion. Its immaculate outcome is ultimately visible in the culmination of the ceremonial year, The Queen's Birthday Parade.

The Major General inspecting Grenadier Guardsmen with eyes sharpened by training and serving on operations to miss nothing.

*The Drill Sergeant
dresses the ranks, while
a Captain corrects
trousers caught on the
Wellington boot of the
Ensign carrying The
Queen's Colour.*

*The Major General
inspects in any weather.*

The Major General
inspecting the battalion
staff; the Pioneer Colour
Sergeant is carrying his
axe of office. By tradition,
Pioneer Sergeants are
the only members of the
British infantry battalions
permitted to wear beards.

The Master Tailor, a
Lance Sergeant,
making adjustments
during the Major
General's inspection
of the Grenadiers.

SPRING DRILLS Drill is a key part of the daily routine of a Foot Guards battalion; it is brought to a pitch of perfection at the start of the year with 'Spring Drills'. During this fortnight the Regimental Sergeant Major and the Drill Sergeants grip the whole battalion and chase it round the square (the Foot Guards barracks' central parade ground) in the evolutions which reach their apogee on Horse Guards in The Queen's Birthday Parade. The experts from the Sergeants' Mess spare no one, not even the most senior officers.

They begin by sizing: 'tallest on the right, shortest on the left, in three ranks, SIZE!' Then they revisit the basics: every aspect of foot drill in slow and quick time is practised, concentrating on keeping down the time to the Foot Guards' 116 paces to the minute, slower and more imposing than the 120 paces of most of the rest of the Army. The pace length is kept to the regulation 30 inches by the pace sticks of the Warrant and senior NCOs, which also measure the distances between ranks and guards.

The focus then shifts to arms drill: rifles for rank and file; sword drill for officers; and for Ensigns, Colour drill. Once up to scratch, they move on to the drill that is the hallmark of the Foot Guards, based on the 'evolutions of the army' – the tactical formations and movements which brought triumph through the centuries. By the end of Spring Drills, each Guardsman is fitter, leaner and stands taller; and each Guard is ready for the specific rehearsals which lead to the Birthday Parade.

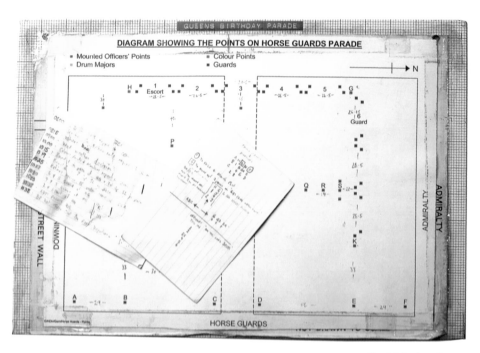

Coldstream Guards rehearsing in Shirt Sleeve Order, marching past the dais in quick time.

The GSM's plan of Horse Guards plus his timing notes. The Parade Square at Pirbright is laid out to simulate Horse Guards. There are markers and the dais.

A Scots Guards drummer beating time at 116 beats per minute.

Grenadier officers drawing swords before marching onto parade.

'Fix Bayonets' – the first movement.

Scots Guards non-commissioned officers drilling.

Grenadiers presenting arms in rehearsal.

The Commanding Officer and the Senior Major riding at the head of his Guards in rehearsal.

Standing at attention.

The Colour Party presenting arms.

The Drill Sergeant giving an officer some personal advice on marching in slow time.

The Ensign flourishing the Colour for rehearsing the March Past in slow time.

THE PREPARATIONS FOR THE BIRTHDAY PARADE: THE HOUSEHOLD CAVALRY

Only one rehearsal for any parade is typically conducted 'on the ground' because of the disruption that bringing over 120 horses through the heart of London entails. To minimise the impact, these rehearsals are completed very early in the morning. Generally first parade will be at 01:30, with somewhat sleepy, bemused horses being led down by equally sleepy Troopers.

It is easy to make mistakes at this unfriendly hour, and the inspection focuses more on safety than on turnout: the Inspecting Officer (the Commanding Officer or Adjutant) is assisted by a farrier (to check the horses' soundness), a saddler (to check the fit of tack), a riding instructor (to check that tack has been applied correctly) and a small team of 'brushers-down' to assist with tightening girths, refitting curb chains and any additional grooming. The Orderly Corporal will note down any faults, and the squadron non-commissioned officers will check that these have been rectified before the parade.

Normally, these rehearsals are conducted in Service Dress Mounted, with khaki jackets and comparatively short leather boots enabling the soldiers to focus on learning their positions, timings and sequencing without having to protect their carefully polished best jackboots. However, where there is a variation in a normal parade, such as an altered route, full State Kit is worn: a man in jackboots is wider than a man in Service Dress, and so a turn that may have seemed manageable in Service Dress becomes a problem in State Kit. Nothing is left to chance.

With a strict time limit to meet before London awakes, the rehearsals have little leeway for readjustments to be made, so much time is spent walking the ground beforehand, picking out markers, measuring distances and ensuring that key personnel understand their roles. Markers are laid out in Hyde Park to replicate the spaces required, and PowerPoint presentations are carefully studied – a combination of low tech and high tech solutions to age-old concerns.

The Household Cavalry early morning inspection at 04:30 hours.

Swords, helmets and gauntlets await their Troopers.

Mounting up for the 04:30 inspection. The Troopers and their horses have already been up for an hour and a half.

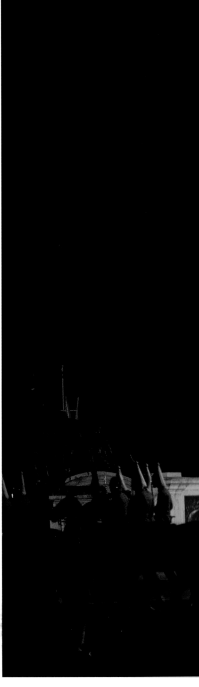

The farriers passing the 'birthday cake' (Queen Victoria Memorial).

Riding over the Serpentine Bridge. It is unusual to be in Mounted Review Order. They are going to rehearse a State Event and need to check their spacings.

The Adjutant takes the salute after the ride out.

The Commanding Officer's horse inspection. The horses have returned from being out to grass over the winter. A Household Cavalry trumpeter's grey is led out for inspection. The cavalry blacks are a minimum of 16.2 hands high, while trumpeters' greys only have to be 16 hands. The horses are reshod every two to six weeks, although some wear through their shoes in just seven days during the ceremonial season.

Finishing touches are applied to a bridle. When the finished bridles leave the saddlers' shop they are buffed and polished by the soldiers every time they are used to maintain their shiny, crisp appearance.

The saddle was last modified in 1902, and takes 60 hours to make by hand. As they are built to last, only about 25 new saddles a year are required. A team of three saddlers is based at the barracks, who make and fix all the leather state uniform for the 260-odd horses and their riders. Each saddle is made specifically for a horse and its name and number are stamped on the back.

The regimental tailors' tasks range from fixing sheepskins for the saddles, to remounting medals, to sewing a button on a tunic. Here one of the tailors trims the plume of a Lance Corporal of The Blues and Royals.

Uniforms are so complicated that the only way to ensure all is in place correctly is through the 'Buddy Buddy' system, whereby Troopers help each other to put on the many elements of kit. Great importance is attached to the uniform and being immaculately turned out.

Squadron Corporal Major's kit inspection.

Captain Archie Horne, The Life Guards, prepares his helmet, which has remained virtually unchanged since modifications in the late 19th century. The helmet is known as the 'Albert' after Queen Victoria's husband, who introduced it in 1842, replacing a bearskin-crested helmet.

The Standard being presented to the Squadron Corporal Major for the daily Queen's Life Guard.

During parades, the Commanding Officer is accompanied by his trumpeter, mounted on a grey horse. In the noise of battle, the trumpeter was the commander's means of communicating orders to the troops. The trumpeters sound the Royal Salute to announce that the Standards are either returning or leaving the barracks. They also sound the trumpet whenever they pass the Palace.

Troopers of The Blues and Royals walk their horses back to the stables.

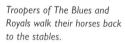

Troopers dismounting in carefully controlled drill. They must show they have freed the bit rein runner (the leather that stops the reins from slipping through the fingers) and that their feet are clear from the stirrups before stepping down.

THE KING'S TROOP When the King's Troop was first created as the Riding Troop in 1946 it moved into the old battery station of St John's Wood. The barracks had only recently been vacated by the Signal Troop and were run-down, but over the next six decades the Wood became synonymous with the King's Troop until it moved to its new state-of-the-art facility at Woolwich Garrison in 2012.

On 6 February of that Diamond Jubilee year the King's Troop formed up on the snowy square in full dress before leaving the Wood for the last time to march to Hyde Park for the firing of a Royal Salute to mark the 60th anniversary of The Queen's accession. Watched by hundreds of local residents, old comrades and well-wishers, a lone trumpeter sounded the last post, the gates were closed, and the Troop marched off down St John's Wood High Street for the final time.

While there were deep feelings of nostalgia for the Wood, the Troop was effectively returning to its artillery roots in Woolwich. The 13-pounder guns were returning to the home of the Royal Arsenal, where they were built, and the Royal Artillery, for whom they were made. Certainly the Troop was made to feel welcome when, at the end of its 12-mile journey, it was cheered by crowds before riding into its new home at King George VI Lines.

This bespoke equestrian facility includes 31,000 square metres of all-weather and grassed training and parade areas, an indoor riding school, stabling for 140 horses, a forge, a saddlery and a gun park. Plans have been approved for a groundbreaking biomass plant that will turn the inevitable by-product of so many horses into heat for the new facilities.

Daily life at Woolwich revolves around the Troop's horses, of course, their care and their training for parade and saluting duties. When young horses begin their careers with the Troop they are partnered with older, more experienced horses as they learn the ropes, with the help of some 20 riding instructors who train both soldiers and horses.

The guns are equally well cared for to keep them in perfect order for Royal Salutes and The Queen's Birthday Parade. Of the Troop's ten 13-pounders only six are on parade at any one time, which allows for one gun to be ready for State funerals, while the remainder undergo maintenance and refurbishment. The intense hours spent applying brass and silver cleaner to the guns' metalwork and 'bliffing' the horses' leatherwork bring glory to the King's Troop and its dedication to the highest standards of horsemanship and military bearing, there for the Sovereign and all to see at the Birthday Parade.

Gunner Leona Gainer polishing the breech. The majority of gun parts can no longer be sourced and so must be hand-machined by soldiers from the Royal Electrical Mechanical Engineers.

*A sub section leaving
Woolwich Barracks for
the arena.*

A sub section doing the scissors at full gallop for the Musical Ride. There are six sub sections, 'A' to 'F': 'A' is positioned Right of the Line, 'D' Centre of the Line and 'F' Left of the Line. It takes many hours of demanding practice to be confident and proficient handling the gun teams.

It takes four to five years to become a fully trained military saddler. The Master Saddler prepares a saddle.

Veterinary Officer Captain Carolyn Whiting from the Royal Army Veterinary Corps tending to a horse. A good horse stays with the Troop for about 12 years but they are all looked at as individuals.

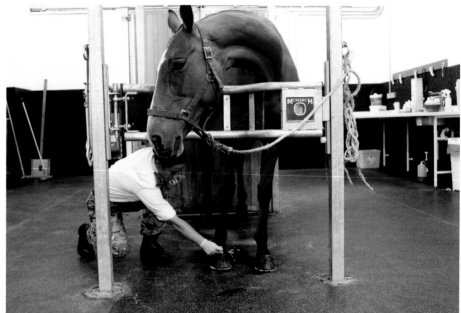

Before a salute or parade, it takes 15 cans of wood polish, seven tubes of metal polish, a can of linseed oil and four cans of penetrating oil to prepare a gun and limber.

On average up to 70 horses a week can be shod at Woolwich's forge, the largest in the Army. The farriers check all the horses on Mondays.

Women were able to
join the King's Troop in
1996 when the Army
opened up most military
occupations to female
soldiers.

Over half of the
members of the King's
Troop are women,
one of the highest
proportions in any unit
of the British Army.

Each horse has two
sets of individually fitted
headcollars, saddles and
harness: a 'bottom' set
for training and a 'top'
set for parades.

Many Gunners have
never ridden before
but develop a lifelong
passion for horses. They
can learn to showjump
and are encouraged to
enter competitions. The
Troop has had several
Olympic showjumping
medallists in its ranks.

THE MASSED BANDS With over 300 musicians on parade, led by the Massed Bands of the Household Division, military music forms an integral part of The Queen's Birthday Parade. The entire parade is best understood as an exercise of several elements carried out in slow and quick march time, with the Trooping the Colour phase forming the centrepiece.

The Massed Bands of the Foot Guards number over 200 musicians and are traditionally accompanied by the Corps of Drums and Pipes and Drums of the battalions on parade. Since 1971 the mounted bands of both regiments of the Household Cavalry have been massed (although this also happened in 1919, 1920 and 1938).

On the announcement of which Foot Guards regiment will have the honour of trooping its Colour, the Senior Director of Music (SDOM) of the Household Division embarks on the process of selecting appropriate music. In January an initial meeting is convened between the respective Regimental Headquarters, Parade Commanding Officer (who will be the Field Officer in Brigade Waiting on the day) and the SDOM to ascertain if there is any specific regimental music to consider and to review previous parades to prevent musical repetition. Thought is also given to any upcoming historical anniversaries (such as Waterloo, the First World War, the Falklands War) that might allow 'musical snapshots' to be referenced. Once the SDOM has all this information, he can plan his musical thoughts and produce a draft programme.

By February, the SDOM has a clear vision of the music for the parade. Meetings will have continued, thoughts discussed and a mutually decided date agreed for an 'audition' to finalise the music. Often, at the request of the regiment or Headquarters Household Division, new music or an apt musical arrangement will be required. As well as having a programme of music prepared for audition, the SDOM must also provide the panel with a list of alternative pieces, should the first choice be rejected.

In March, the panel convenes to audition all proposed music for The Queen's Birthday Parade. The panel is chaired by the Major General, assisted by the Brigade Major, representation from the regiment and the Garrison Sergeant Major. A single Foot Guards band is tasked to perform the music, traditionally the band that the SDOM commands. To add reality, a large television screen is placed in front of the panel, playing back a recording of a previous parade.

With the volume muted, the band performs the suggested music mirroring the exact sequence of the parade. Should the SDOM's nominated piece be deemed unsuitable, the panel asks to hear the alternatives. Should these also fail to please, the SDOM must investigate further pieces for a second audition. Very occasionally even a third audition can be required to consolidate the final music programme.

The panel scrutinises several criteria for each piece of music before making its

*Full band practice for
The Queen's Birthday
Parade on the square at
Wellington Barracks.*

The Senior Director of Music Lieutenant Colonel Kevin Roberts rehearsing with the Band of the Welsh Guards in one of the practice rooms at Wellington Barracks. When the programme of music has been chosen, it is performed in the Guards' Chapel in front of the Major General. Once he is satisfied, the choices are finally sent to The Queen for her approval.

final decision: appropriateness; regimental affiliation; length; volume; and, most importantly when selecting the March Past quick and slow marches, if divisions will be able to hear a consistent, solid tempo. Given the substantial area of Horse Guards, the latter is critical for the Garrison Sergeant Major. Once the final decision is made, a definitive list is issued to the Foot Guards Central Music Library and work begins to produce music parts for every musician.

During The Queen's Inspection phase of the parade, the Massed Bands play slow and quick music. Performed while stationary, this is the only opportunity during the parade when the Massed Bands can perform the most demanding music. Timing of these pieces is crucial to allow for an effective musical cut-off.

While at certain points it is possible for the Massed Bands and the Household Cavalry Band to feature new repertoire, several pieces are considered 'traditional' and are therefore repeated.

Arguably the most poignant and memorable moment of the parade comes straight after the verbal order 'Troop', where, following a haunting crescendo and diminuendo held chord, the Massed Bands step off in slow time to the spectacular 'Les Huguenots' waltz. From the 1836 opera by Giacomo Meyerbeer, this ever popular slow march, a firm favourite with the Massed Bands, was played frequently on the parade from 1869 and has been used every year at this point since 1937.

Full band practice with the Pipes and Drums of the Scots Guards for The Queen's Birthday Parade on the square at Wellington Barracks.

The State Trumpeters practising fanfares.

Putting on the kettledrums simultaneously to avoid overbalancing even the mighty drum horses.

Rehearsals for The Queen's Birthday Parade on the square at Horse Guards. Note how the reins are held when playing different instruments. Horses are sorted to be suitable for the band; the older and more experienced horses are used and they never have to trot on parade.

UNIFORMS The living participants in The Queen's Birthday Parade belong to two species: *Homo sapiens* and *Equus ferus* (plus in any year when the Irish Guards troop their Colour, one solitary *Canis lupus familiaris*, the Irish Wolfhound mascot that leads the regiment onto parade). There is, however, a virtual menagerie of creatures great and small that contributes in other ways, providing the materials for the uniforms and accoutrements that grace the parade.

Perhaps the most famous of these are the bearskin caps of the Foot Guards. Photographs and paintings of Victorian Guardsmen suggest that their caps were larger and finer than those of today. This can be attributed to the commercial instincts of the hunters and trappers who killed the bears when they were at their fattest and sleekest, just before hibernation. Originally, like their French Imperial Guard prototypes, the caps were made from the pelts of the Eurasian Brown Bear, which was widely distributed in continental Europe. The main source of supply was Russia, until the Crimean War, since which they have come from Canada, from pelts of the American Black Bear. Some 40,000 of these bears are killed annually, most culled in licensed hunting in North America; a small fraction are killed on the roads. Some 50 pelts a year are used to sustain the stock of British bearskins and each pelt makes at least one cap. The officers' ones, which are taller, are traditionally made from the more luxuriant fur of the female bear.

Bearskin caps have cane or bamboo frames, over which two pieces of fur, for front and back, are stitched. There is an inner leather adjustable head lining which is individually fitted to the wearer. Each bearskin has leather slots for plumes on both sides, so it can be worn by members of all five regiments. The curb chain of brass rings, graduated from the centre, on leather backing is not a chinstrap: worn under the lower lip, it acts as a counterweight, helping to keep the cap in place, especially in windy conditions. Every man on parade is assigned his own bearskin cap and when he leaves the service they are handed in for reuse. The vast majority of bearskins on parade are around 50 years old, having been repeatedly reconditioned and returned to service. Some bearskins are far older; that worn by the Colonel of the Coldstream Guards is said to have been holed by a Russian musket ball at the Alma, making it over 165 years old.

The shape of the bearskin differs, in many cases, for officers and other ranks. From the front, a soldier's should look rather like an apple, while an officer's appears more pear shaped, with a slightly concave front, although in recently made bearskins it is harder to discern this difference. The depth of the officer's cap is 11.5 inches in front and 16 inches at the back, while the soldier's is 9 inches in front and 13.5 inches at the back.

The King's Troop busby was also originally made from bearskin but changed to

The high collar and gauntlets protect from sword cuts.

sealskin later in the 1800s, and the plume is made from ostrich feathers. Its red flap was designed to be filled with sand to protect against the swipes of enemy sabres, although military wisdom also has it that the 'busby bag' was useful for storing love letters.

The headdress worn by the Household Cavalry is known as the Albert Helmet. With styles of helmet changing frequently, and increasing in size to ridiculous proportions as officers sought to cut a dash, in 1842 Prince Albert designed a more practical helmet for both regiments to wear. The Life Guards have white plumes, and The Blues and Royals have red, while farriers of The Life Guards wear black plumes. These are all now made of horsehair, but there are still some made from the original materials: yak hair for The Blues and Royals, and whalebone for The Life Guards.

Both now sound extraordinary, but in earlier times the materials were chosen for simple utility. Yak hair is still prized and used widely in the Himalayas and their foothills for its strength and resistance to extreme weather. Whalebone, or to be more precise baleen, is made from the filter-feeding system of baleen whales; bristle-like strips of keratin, baleen has qualities of plasticity and impermeability which made it the natural predecessor of plastics. From the late 18th century it was widely used to make the ribs of corsets; the process of making them into uniform strips produced shavings that were sold to

milliners to decorate hats with artificial plumes that were rain-resistant.

Baleen is no longer used. Instead, all of the modern Household Cavalry plumes, including those known as 'beards' that hang from the throat lash of all Blues and Royals horses and the drum horses of both regiments (originally to protect horses' throats from sword cuts in battle), are made from horsehair, as are the plumes of non-commissioned officers and Guardsmen in all the Foot Guards regiments.

Grenadiers of all ranks wear horsehair plumes; in the other regiments, the officers' and Warrant Officers' plumes are made of goose feathers. The Major General and some of the officers of the Royal Household and general staff wear cocked hats, whose plumes are made of swans' feathers. The cocked hat originated from the early tricorn hat of the infantry soldier. In order for a grenadier to throw his grenade, he had to sling his firelock across his back, invariably knocking off his hat. Very quickly the tricorn hat had its sides cocked up to avoid this problem, and the cocked hat evolved from this adaptation, to be worn much later by officers.

Although the Scots Guards wear no plumes in their bearskins, there are three types of plume in the regiment: pipers wear red and blue goose feather plumes in their bonnets, which are themselves made of ostrich feathers; Scots Guards Quartermasters wear white duck feather plumes in their cocked hats; and The

Jerk leather became jackboots. Their height protects from sword cuts. The cuirasses came from the French cavalry after Waterloo. The epaulettes and the straps add protection. The Life Guards have an 'onion' on top of their plume.

The hat was designed to serve also as a bucket. It is attached to the uniform by busby lines. The plume could have been a shaving brush held tight by a Gunner's wedding ring. The frogging was a form of body armour.

Queen wore a black goose feather cockade in her headdress as Colonel-in-Chief of the regiment, which matches the relevant coloured ones that she wore as Colonel-in-Chief of each of the other Guards regiments.

The buff belts of the Guardsmen, boots and most of the saddlery and other horse furniture are made from cowhide; but other animal hides are used for a wide range of other items. The buckskin breeches of the Household Cavalry were originally made of deer hide, but sheep leather is now more commonly used. Their gauntlets, and the gloves of Foot Guards officers, are made of kid or goatskin. Life Guards officers' shabraques (saddlecloths) are lined in doeskin and black Morocco, fine goatskin or sheepskin; their 'flounces', worn over the saddle, are white goatskin; those of The Blues and Royals, black lambskin. Other ranks of both regiments have sheepskin flounces, white for The Life Guards and black for The Blues and Royals. The white leather crossbelt of the Household Cavalry formerly functioned as a spare girth, while the red flask cord carried a gunpowder flask. The back of the belt holds a cartouche box, the design of which has not changed since 1856. Originally used to carry powder and shot for flintlock weapons, they became merely ornamental with the introduction of breech-loading carbines. They are, however, the perfect place to keep a mobile phone – switched off, of course.

The sword handles of the Household Cavalry and the Foot Guards are made of shagreen – sharkskin, with its unique gripping qualities. Those of general officers were traditionally of ivory; new ones are made from bone.

So a great variety of hide and feather from a veritable Noah's Ark of creatures has contributed over the years to the uniforms worn on the Sovereign's Birthday Parade; but the most numerous by far to give its all for the ceremonial is an insect – the humble silkworm. As well as the dresses, scarves and ties of the watching crowds, they provide the silk of which the Standards and Colours of the regiments are woven, and the sashes worn by the Foot Guards officers. The 2,000 to 3,000 cocoons required for each pound of silk make *Bombyx mori* overwhelmingly the greatest contributor species to the parade, although it is far from the most recognised.

No account of the uniforms so proudly on display in the Birthday Parade would be complete without mention of the gold braid that is a feature in some way on every parading participant, but most noticeably in the cavalry units. The braid worn by officers and non-commissioned officers is a reflection of the past practice of a commander carrying enough rope to secure the number of horses for which he was responsible. The increasing level of braid worn at different ranks stops at Troop Leader, otherwise the Commanding Officer would not be able to move for the weight.

Dismounted Review Order. The thin red line of the cartouche belt is from a flash cord. The aiguillettes had two purposes: spiking a gun or banging into the ground to hobble a horse.

… and a pear behind.'

*The 13 studs represent the
13 Victoria Crosses won by
the Guards regiments in
the Crimea.*

BOOT PREPARATION
by Guardsman Hollis, Grenadier Guards

First stage
New boots are filled with damp sand and laced up tight using wire.

Second stage
Several hours later beeswax is melted into the leather, a process known as burning down.

Third stage
When the boots have cooled down, the sand is taken out and excess wax is taken off. Black polish is then rubbed in until there is no evidence of the grain of the leather.

Fourth stage
Polish is massaged in then polished off, preferably with a Selvyt cloth, and rubbed in again. This process is repeated and can take from one to three hours.

Fifth stage
Soldiers wear the boots until they fit their feet. Marching in them is the best way to achieve a good fit.

Every time the parade boots are worn they have to be re-polished. Damage is caused by marching through horse manure, dust and gravel and standing in the sun. Boots are recycled and there are boots still being worn that date back to 1969. Many Guardsmen are thus much younger than their boots. The leather and stitching of the old boots is better than the modern boots, but today's boots have a shock absorber in the heel. Band members have rubber soles on some of their boots for when they are performing indoors.

DRUM MAJORS, PIPERS AND DRUMMERS

'A Drumme is one of the necessariest officers… hee ought to be a man of personage, faithful, secret and trusty.' *The Principles of the Art Militarie* by Henry Hexham (1637).

It is unthinkable to countenance The Queen's Birthday Parade without the rousing sound of drums. Their beat instils into the soldier the swing of the movement of marching rather than the action of walking – crucial when so many soldiers are moving together in close formation.

Yet until the Crusaders brought back the notion of the drum as a military aid, having witnessed its use by the Saracens, only the bugle and the trumpet had been heard on the battlefield by English soldiers. In 1347 Edward III's triumphant entry into Calais was led by drummers, and by the time Henry VIII entered Boulogne in 1544 with his drummers, their role in State Ceremonial was firmly established. Drummers were placed around the Standards in battle and as long as they kept beating, soldiers were reassured that the Standards were safe, even if hidden from view in the melee.

Though the title Drum Major appears in older records, it was not introduced as a true rank until 1810. Previously, Drum Majors had been paid simply as drummers, although in practice they had long enjoyed the status and pay of Sergeants. Deductions from the pay of the other drummers made up the difference, but in 1810 this inequitable arrangement ceased when Drum Majors were granted the actual rank and pay of Sergeants. The appointment of Drum Major is no longer restricted to Sergeants, as Colour Sergeants and Warrant Officers often become Drum Majors. The appointment is made by Royal Warrant, thus is a Royal Household appointment, not an Army one.

By the 1700s the role took on a more punitive aspect, since courts martial were often held

The Senior Drum Major in State Dress.

The Coldstream Drum Major in Home Service Clothing.

The Pipe Major of the Band of the Scots Guards wears the Royal Stewart tartan and the black ostrich feather bonnet of the Pipes and Drums. Five tails hang down to denote the five regiments. The privilege of wearing these bonnets with their red and blue feather plume was granted by King George V in 1926. The three tails on the sporran represent the three original Guards regiments.

When wearing spats which have 16 buttons the total number of buttons is 42; 1642 is the date on which the regiment was raised. All military pipers must complete the Piping Course at the Army School of Bagpipe Music and Highland Drumming in Edinburgh. Pipe Majors undergo the intensive 28-week All Arms Pipe Majors' Course, culminating in a final test judged by prestigious members of the Piobaireachd Society.

Most pipers wear silver buckles on their shoes, but not the pipers of the Irish Guards. In 1916, when the pipers were formed, their brogue shoes were not ready for their first performance. In haste the shoemaker cut down some boots, making the extended tongue, but couldn't find any buckles. The style stuck. The beret is called a caubeen, worn with the St Patrick's blue plume.

The first 12 pipers were trained by the London Irish Rifles. Later the Guards pipers moved their cap badge to the right side of the caubeen in tribute to the London Irish who also wear theirs on the right side. The saffron kilt is fastened on the right side of the over apron by two round green felt circles with small Celtic brooches that are used in place of a kilt pin. Irish Guards pipers originally played the Great Irish Warpipes, a two-drone version of the three-drone Great Highland Bagpipe. In 1968, however, the Highland pipe was standardised throughout the Army and has been used by the Irish Guards ever since.

Irish Guards Lance Corporal in the Pipe Band.

Scots Guards Pipe Major has a blue bag.

on the battlefield using the drum head as the court table. The Drum Major not only superintended floggings of soldiers but also had to instruct the drummers to flog with both hands. Sometimes, however, it was the drummer who was flogged.

One drummer received 25,000 lashes in the 14 years he served in Gibraltar in the early 1700s.

Originally the senior drummer wore only a standard pattern leather drummer's carriage fitted with loops to secure the drumsticks when not in use. When the Drum Major's appointment was authorised, his shoulder belt retained the drumsticks and loops, but gained embellishments such as the regimental badge and Battle Honours.

Gradually the drumsticks became smaller to make room for the embellishments until today the ebony sticks, although essentially a part of the ceremonial baldric, stand as a symbol of the original appointment.

Today's Drum Majors play a prominent role in co-ordinating the formations of the Birthday Parade, as well as enhancing its pageantry with their Restoration-era Gold Coats, the oldest surviving uniform in the British Army.

In 1997 the Director of Infantry instituted the Cutlers' Sword competition to identify the drummer or bugler who has shown the commitment, skill and potential to become a future Senior Drum Major or Bugle Major. Since its inception, seven Foots Guards drummers have been awarded an 1895 pattern drummer's sword, donated by the Worshipful Company of Cutlers, which they may carry on parade in ceremonial uniform.

It is presented by the Lord Mayor of London at the Lord Mayor's Show.

After the defeat of the French at the Battle of Blenheim on 13 August 1704, the captured French Colours were handed to General John Churchill, 1st Duke of Marlborough, when he received the surrender from Marshal Tallard. To commemorate this important victory in the War of the Spanish Succession, the duke adopted the fleur de lys as his motif and since then British Army drummers have worn the fleur de lys on their jackets. The arrangement of stripes on the tunics of the Guards drummers matches the arrangement of buttons according to their regiments.

Scots Guards Sergeant in the Corps of Drums.

Coldstream Guards drummer. The white hat band and drum trim reflect the Puritan origins of Monck's Regiment of Foot, the antecedent of the Coldstream Guards.

Scots Guards Corporal in the Regimental Band.

THE PRINCESS ELIZABETH CUP As skilled equestrians, the Royal Family are enthusiastic supporters of the Royal Windsor Horse Show, held annually in the Windsor Home Park. King George VI and Queen Elizabeth attended the first show in 1944 and watched the Princesses Elizabeth and Margaret win prizes in front of 8,000 spectators. Since then several members of the Royal Family have competed, and until fairly recently Prince Philip competed in carriage-driving events.

One of the most anticipated events in the show is the presentation by Her Majesty of the Princess Elizabeth Cup to the 'Best Turned Out Trooper'. This immaculate soldier, astride an equally spotless horse, has been judged to be the man whose turnout is the very best in the Household Cavalry Mounted Regiment. Turnout is very important in a ceremonial regiment; every day the soldiers who are to form The Queen's Life Guard are inspected, with those judged to be the smartest allocated the prime positions in the mounted sentry boxes in Whitehall. It tends to be from these soldiers, or 'boxmen', that the competitors for the Princess Elizabeth Cup are drawn.

Judging starts well before the show. Each of the six Troops nominates two representatives. They then carefully select a horse that will stand patiently during a long inspection, and, crucially, that has a set of tack that will polish up well. While all the Troop lends a hand, it is the competitors who bear the brunt of the extraordinary degree of kit preparation required. Long hours are devoted to 're-waxing' (coating the leather in beeswax) and polishing every piece of the head kit, or bridle, and the saddle, stirrup leathers and girth to a remarkable standard and with no detail overlooked.

Judging is based on the marking format used on the daily Queen's Life Guard inspection, but the level of detail required to catch the judges' eyes is minute – every stitch will be individually picked out, every surface made perfectly smooth, every hair combed into place. The horses and men are wrapped in sheets as the kit is put on to prevent any dust from settling, which are then whipped off as the inspection begins to reveal the brilliant shine underneath.

The judging team consists of the Commanding Officer, Adjutant and Regimental Corporal Major, assisted by the Garrison Sergeant Major and two invited guests. They inspect each entrant individually and then agree an aggregate score. The top four from each squadron are then selected to be presented to The Queen at the show, with the winner being announced as she makes her inspection. All eight have the added reward of representing the regiment at the Canadian International Horse Show later in the year. Finally these eight soldiers form the Retinue on The Queen's Birthday Parade; four escort the Brigade Major as he leads the whole parade up The Mall, and four bring up the rear with the Regimental Adjutant. They then spend the parade either side of Her Majesty's dais, an honoured position that demands very patient horses.

The Queen has a particular interest in this competition and in personally presenting the prize. It is evidence of another close bond that she has forged with the aspiration for excellence in her Household Cavalry Troopers.

A Trooper entering the
Princess Elizabeth Cup
being helped by a friend.
All Troopers need help
to dress and do so in
accordance with the
'Buddy Buddy' system.

Chalking, painting and
polishing the hooves.

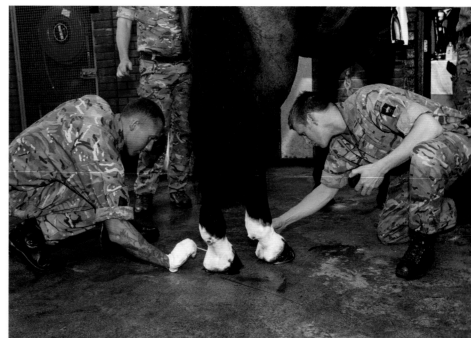

Helping the Trooper
mount without
getting anything dirty
or damaged.

Every part of the
horse, harness and the
Trooper's uniform is
meticulously checked
by the judges.

The horses are lovingly prepared to look their very best.

Protecting Trooper Harrison Chapple, the eventual winner.

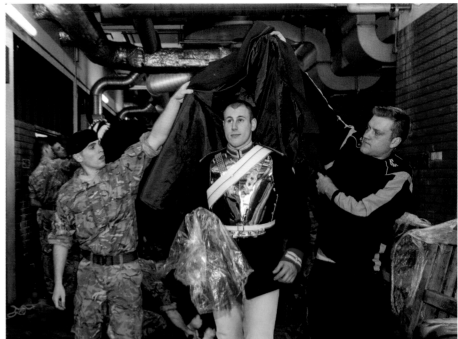

The Garrison Sergeant Major checking the whiteness of the inside of the boot.

Sergeant Major David Lochrie inspecting the harness with the checklist.

In order to demonstrate the excellent standards of horsemanship achieved in the Household Cavalry Mounted Regiment, and to encourage soldiers to develop their riding beyond the demands of parade, the regiment's display team tours the country and the world. Its carefully choreographed display of formation riding, with stunts involving jumping crossed lances, horses lying down on command and intricate manoeuvres conducted at speed to music, is a brilliant tool for developing the confidence and skill of horse and rider. With recent displays in Switzerland and Oman, as well as in front of audiences at home, the Musical Ride helps raise the profile of the British Army while providing spectacular entertainment. Considering that over 90 per cent of soldiers have never ridden before they join the regiment, the standard achieved is remarkable.

The Musical Drive is the
final event of the day,
after which the King's
Troop fire their guns.
They then close the
show by galloping out of
the arena.

BEATING RETREAT On the Wednesday and Thursday evenings before The Queen's Birthday Parade a sunset pageant of precision drill, horses, cannons and fireworks is performed to the accompaniment of rousing military music. Known as 'Beating Retreat', this dramatic display of pageantry in Horse Guards Parade has pragmatic origins.

The roots of Beating Retreat lie in the original purpose of military music – to assist war. While today's battlefield commanders pass orders using state-of-the-art communications, their forebears merely instructed a drummer, a trumpeter or a bugler to beat or sound a particular call. Similarly, before clocks and wristwatches were commonplace, drum beating or trumpet/bugle calls regulated a soldier's life both in and outside barracks. 'Retreat' can be traced back to the earliest records of British conflicts when, as darkness fell, a signal was given to instruct troops to break off fighting and return to their lines.

The term was further enshrined in Humphrey Bland's widely used 1727 *Treatise of Military Discipline*, which stated: 'Half an hour before the gates are to be shut, generally at the setting of the sun, the Drummers of the Port Guards are to go upon the ramparts and beat a Retreat to give notice that the gates are to be shut.'

The Duke of Cumberland, who put down the Jacobite rebellion of 1745, distinguished between 'Retreat' and 'Tattoo' when he ordered: 'The Retreat is to beat at Sunset and the Tattoo is to be beat at a later hour as ordered by the Commandants of individual encampments.' Nowadays, marching displays are centred around the dual traditions of beating 'Retreat' and 'Tattoo'.

London District Beating Retreats and Tattoos have been held on Horse Guards Parade since the end of the Second World War as the Government hoped that the sight of the Foot Guards back in full ceremonial dress would help to inspire the nation after years of wartime austerity. These annual performances were held on Saturday evenings and included: Musical Drive of the King's Troop, Royal Horse Artillery; Musical Ride of the Household Cavalry; Massed Bands of the Household Division; and Drums and Pipes of the Brigade of Guards.

In its current form, the Beating Retreat by the Household Division has taken place since 1966 and raises money for Household Division Charities and other service good causes. From 1977 until 1998, it was held later in the evening, illuminated by soldiers of the Territorial Army using searchlights retained from the war. In 1999 it shifted back to late afternoon, but with the introduction of professional floodlighting in 2009, it returned to the evening, with the addition of a large television screen to enhance the audience's view of the spectacle and its glorious setting. Usually, on at least one of the evenings, a senior member of the Royal Family takes the salute.

The kettledrums, weighing around 25kg each, are strapped on tightly enough so that they don't fall, but with enough play to allow the horses to move. The drummers steer with reins attached to the stirrups: a great act of trust as they are not in a strong position to react if their horses shy.

The Musical Drive of
the King's Troop, Royal
Horse Artillery. They
are coming out of the
scissors movement.
'Bonnie Dundee' is the
principal music as the
Troop enters and exits
the arena.

*An American
military choir.*

*Pipers of the Irish and
Scots Guards flank
a Reservist from the
London Scottish.*

Two guns of the King's
Troop fire rounds in
the finale.

The lone piper.

The Senior Director of Music
and his French counterpart.

The Massed Bands, the
French Bands of the Troupes
de Marine and the Légion
Étrangère (the French
Foreign Legion) and the
Vancouver Police Pipe Band.

HORSE GUARDS

HORSE GUARDS Horse Guards Parade is the theatrical arena for Trooping the Colour, shaped for this purpose over the centuries. The land was once part of the London residence of the Archbishops of York. Henry VIII appropriated the building from Cardinal Wolsey, naming it Whitehall Palace. Close by was a tilting field for knights to hold tournaments; Elizabeth I held two annual tournaments here to mark her accession and her birthday.

After the Restoration, Charles II needed barracks for his first Standing Army, consisting of the Household Cavalry and two Foot Guards regiments. A redbrick structure was put up on the Tiltyard, with stabling for 100 horses and Foot Guards billets. The division of two important parishes was marked through the building's centre. A line on the ceiling of the current arch shows the border between St Margaret's Westminster and St Martin-in-the-Fields.

In 1745 George II ordered the construction of a new Horse Guards Building. Naturally, it contains the vital archway entrance to the royal estate at its centre; above is the oval topped window into the Levee Room, intended as the base for the Commander-in-Chief. The Palladian west face is topped by a cupola containing the clock, whose three bells can be heard at the point the monarch arrives for Trooping.

The four-storey west front sits central to Horse Guards Parade and provides the symmetrical backdrop to The Queen's saluting base. The roof line has a balustrade to reveal the crowning cupola and clock, with the blackened Roman numeral II to remind all of the regicide committed within feet of this place, when Charles I was executed at 2pm on 30 January 1649.

The Levee Room is now the Major General's office. From its splendid Venetian window members of the Royal Family watch the parade. The Prince Consort did so, in Queen Victoria's absence, and witnessed the Commander-in-Chief, the Duke of Wellington, take the salute. The Iron Duke's desk is still kept in the room where he worked and is used by the Major General.

Laid out before the Horse Guards Building is the arena for the nation's principal annual ceremonial, which encompasses in a gravelled square what is left of the Tiltyard.

Horse Guards Parade and Building are purpose built to be the logical place for the Guard Change, regularly for The Queen's Life Guard and in the summer for the Palace Foot Guards. These ceremonies are all part of the preparation for the two reviews that finally ready the Household Division for The Queen's Birthday Parade. For the rest of the year, the building is a busy HQ for the Household Division, with its nationwide ceremonial responsibilities, and London District, with specific responsibilities for the provision of civil contingency in the capital.

Horse Guards from Whitehall, one of the tourist sights of London. Mounted guards are changed every hour, dismounted every second hour. This rests the horses, and incentivises a high standard of turnout: the best four in the inspection prior to the Guard Mount are those who carry out the mounted guards, while the dismounted duties are taken by the remainder.

An officer rides from Knightsbridge every day arriving at 16:00 to inspect the Guard at Horse Guards. Queen Victoria ordered this to happen for 100 years as a punishment when the Guard failed to 'turn out' for her once, and the tradition continues.
Captain Rob Perera, The Blues and Royals, going out for an early morning ride.

THE GUARDS DIVISION MEMORIAL The United Kingdom first determined to honour the memory of every one of its war dead, permanently and by name, after the Great War. Previously, memorials had been occasional or just personal to one individual among many, picked out by a grieving family. Social change, wrought by altered expectations after the war, demanded something different.

Although George V had been unwilling to support the planned temporary wooden cenotaph for the 1920 funeral of the Unknown Warrior, he soon realised the strength of feeling that demanded it be replaced in Portland stone for the following year. Sir Edwin Lutyens's structure embodied in its proportions and lines the eternities demanded by a wounded nation.

This was what the Guards Division wanted too. By 1926 its memorial had been completed to a design by Harold Chalton Bradshaw, one of the foremost designers of war memorials: a broad obelisk in Portland stone on a podium with a three-stepped plinth. Bronze Guardsmen of the five regiments, modelled on five survivors of the war, stand easy along the raised platform on the east side, facing Horse Guards. Depicted in Battle Order, rather than Order of Precedence, they are: Sergeant R Bradshaw MM, Grenadier Guards; Guardsman J McDonald, Scots Guards; Guardsman A Comley, Welsh Guards; Guardsman S McCarthy, Irish Guards; and Lance Corporal J S Richardson, Coldstream Guards. The legs for the figure modelled by Guardsman McCarthy are, in fact, those of Lance Sergeant W J Kidd, who took over the pose when McCarthy allegedly walked off.

Rudyard Kipling served the memory of his Irish Guards son John, who was obliterated by a shell in the Battle of Loos. Kipling wrote the inscription for the memorial: 'To the Glory of God and in the memory of the Officers Warrant Officers Non Commissioned Officers & Guardsmen of His Majesty's Regiments of Foot Guards who gave their lives for their King and Country during the Great War 1914–1918... in the fight for the World's Freedom.' An additional carved dedication was made to those lost in the war against Hitler and fascism and the words encompass all those lost since.

The memorial was unveiled with religious blessings before Field Marshal the Duke of Connaught, Senior Colonel of the Guards Division, on 16 October 1926. Among those present was the 100-year-old former Grenadier and Crimea veteran General George Higginson.

The hunger of the German machine guns and the unremitting cold, wet and barbed wire are set in the faces of the remembering Guardsmen but it was a world away from the scarlet ceremonial of this ancient parade ground. The siting of this memorial directly before the gaze of the Sovereign at Trooping the Colour was deliberate: this was where Guardsman and Sovereign came eye to eye annually and their memory would live for an eternity of monarchs.

The markers march on to Horse Guards Parade past the Guards Division Memorial at the beginning of The Queen's Birthday Parade, carrying Company Colours. The dominating backdrop of the parade is the Memorial, a sentinel promise to honour the Sovereign, protect freedom and Remember the Dead.

The bronze for the statues of the five Guardsmen was taken from German guns captured by the Guards Division. Damage caused to the Guards Division Memorial during the Blitz can be seen on the Portland stone. The shell damage was left largely unrepaired, some say on Winston Churchill's express direction.

THE MAJOR GENERAL As the Royal Procession makes its way onto Horse Guards Parade, no one bears more responsibility for the day than the officer riding behind the Regimental Colonels. Mounted by custom on a grey charger, with aiguillettes on his right shoulder denoting his membership of the Royal Household, and his scarlet tunic and cocked hat that he is a serving general officer, he is known to all members of the Household Division simply as the Major General.

His full title is more ponderous: General Officer Commanding London District and Major General Commanding the Household Division. He exercises both commands from London's finest office, sitting at the Duke of Wellington's magnificent oval desk in the great room over the Horse Guards arch, once the office of the Commander-in-Chief.

Command of the Household Troops has evolved over the centuries. Nearly a year after his Restoration, Charles II signed the Royal Warrant that authorised his personal troops on 26 January 1661, effectively founding today's British Army: 'His Majesty's own Troop of Guards, His Highness Royal the Duke of York his Troop of Guards, His Grace the Duke of Albermarle his Troop of Guards' (all now The Life Guards); 'The Royal Regiment of Horse' (today's Blues and Royals); 'The King's Royal Regiment of Foot Guards' (now the Grenadier Guards); and 'The Lord General's Regiment of Foot Guards' (today the Coldstream Guards).

Each regiment was technically commanded by its Colonel, but the effective tactical and administrative units were Troops (in the infantry, Companies), commanded by Captains. The term 'battalion' for a grouping of Companies on active service was not introduced until 1686; when formed, they were usually commanded by Lieutenant Colonels. In 1715, largely to cut costs, battalion commanders were reduced to the rank of Major, although one Lieutenant Colonel was retained to act in lieu of the Colonel, commanding the regiment as well as one of the battalions. The Lieutenant Colonels commanding Foot Guards battalions in London took it in turns to be on duty at Court, to receive and transmit royal orders to the Foot Guards, with the title of Field Officer in Brigade Waiting. This gave the Lieutenant Colonels effective command over the Brigade of Guards, since all orders for them were issued by this means until 1856, when the Adjutant General wrote to Major General Lord Rokeby, who had commanded the Guards Brigade in the Crimean War: 'Her Majesty has been graciously pleased to appoint you to serve upon the staff, with a view to your exercising a general supervision over all the battalions of the Guards in England… Your Headquarters will be in London, and all communications having reference to the Guards are to be addressed to your Lordship instead of the Field Officer in Brigade Waiting.'

Major General Christopher Ghika, late Irish Guards, standing in his office overlooking Horse Guards Parade Square. The Duke of Wellington's desk is on the left.

This order created the appointment of the Major General; in the same year his command, the Foot Guards, were designated a Division. These developments were not universally welcomed. The Commander-in-Chief, arch-conservative the Duke of Cambridge, wrote orders for Lord Rokeby that proved unworkable. After two years Rokeby recommended the abolition of the Lieutenant Colonels, an issue so contentious, and the influence of Guards Officers so considerable, that it was only settled by a mere three votes in the House of Commons in favour of retaining the Major General's appointment.

Changes continued. In 1868 the Foot Guards were redesignated the Brigade of Guards; in 1869 the Army-reforming Secretary of State for War, Lord Cardwell, proposed that the Major General should become 'General of the London District'. The power of the Lieutenant Colonels over their regiments still endured, however. In March that year Cardwell announced to the House: 'There are in the regiments of Guards not only a General in command of the whole Brigade but also a Lieutenant Colonel… who is… at the head of a brigade within a brigade, and is Lieutenant Colonel of the Regiment… We do not propose that the separate command of Lieutenant Colonel of a regiment should be continued but that a Lieutenant Colonel in the Guards should command his own battalion.' This meant that one battalion in each regiment was commanded by a Lieutenant Colonel, the others by Majors. Cardwell had achieved at least a modicum of economy – financially, if not linguistically.

More change followed in 1875, when Volunteer Forces were introduced, organised in London into three brigades. The three Foot Guards Regimental Lieutenant Colonels were restored to command them as Brigadiers; and in 1881 a Royal Warrant declared that the Majors commanding battalions were to be Lieutenant Colonels. These arrangements largely endured until 1988, when the role of Regimental Lieutenant Colonel ceased to be a full time appointment, but was vested in a senior serving or retired officer. They still retain moral responsibility for their regiments, as does the Commander Household Cavalry, whose position has followed a path at least as tortuous. The greatest development had come in December 1950, when George VI directed that the Household Cavalry should come under the command of the Major General Commanding the Household Brigade – since 1967 the Household Division.

Through all this the Major General survives, still responsible for London District and the Household Division, with the same responsibilities for troops and military activity as any other British commander, including security and other civil support tasks. In addition he is responsible for all the ceremonial duties and events in London and Windsor, as well as for all matters pertaining to the values and standards of the Household Division wherever in the world its members are serving. In these matters he is responsible to their Colonel-in-Chief – the Sovereign.

The Major General riding Merlin behind The Queen and the Colonels during the Inspection at the start of The Queen's Birthday Parade.

THE BRIGADE MAJOR The Brigade Major's post has been established on the permanent staff at Headquarters Household Division at Horse Guards since 1861 and since then a total of 72 officers have held the post. The current incumbent knows the exact number, as photographs of each of his predecessors gaze down on him from his office wall with expressions ranging from benign encouragement to sneering disapproval.

The Brigade Major is the senior London District planning officer and spends the vast majority of his time ensuring that State Ceremonial and Public Duties are delivered to the highest standards and that the troops assigned to them have all of the support that they need. He has, in HQ Household Division, itself a part of HQ London District, a strong and knowledgeable team which includes the Garrison Sergeant Major and the Superintendent Clerk, two of the Army's most senior and experienced Warrant Officers who, between them, know almost everything there is to know about organising and performing ceremonial duties.

Should their knowledge fail them they consult the Household Division Standing Orders, a weighty tome which has evolved over many years to provide detailed direction on all aspects of the organisation, responsibilities and procedures for all general duties and training and the conduct of the Royal Guards and all ceremonial events, including The Queen's Birthday Parade. The Standing Orders are always only *mostly* up to date, and circumstances in the modern military environment change so fast that there is always room for interpretation. This task also falls to the Brigade Major; with the need to balance tradition with the wishes of the Royal Household, the Army, the public expectation and the officers and men of the Household Division, it is a continuous challenge but constantly rewarding and great fun.

In preparation for The Queen's Birthday Parade, the Brigade Major has the responsibility of supervising the 'Guard Mounts from Horse Guards' – the series of dress rehearsals which allow the Garrison Sergeant Major and other seniors to assess the results of training at Pirbright and to fine tune the performance of the Guards before the Major General's Review. On the day of the parade itself the Brigade Major has the honour of leading Her Majesty The Queen's procession from Buckingham Palace to Horse Guards Parade and ensuring that her coachman can deliver her to the dais for precisely 11:00.

*Brigade Major
Lieutenant Colonel
Guy Stone, Welsh
Guards, in the Rotunda
over the arch at Horse
Guards.*

WO1 Sergeant Major Lee Hutt, Coldstream Guards, Superintending Clerk of the Household Division; Staff Sergeant Ilaitia Vuki AGC (SPS). They are responsible for issuing the co-ordinating instructions and administering the tickets to the two Reviews and The Queen's Birthday Parade. Tickets for the parade are eight times oversubscribed and are issued by ballot. Preparations for the parade and Beating Retreat start in January.

Garrison Sergeant Major
London District A J (Vern)
Stokes under the arch of
Horse Guards with the
Guards Memorial beyond the
parade ground.

THE GARRISON SERGEANT MAJOR Carved into most soldiers' memories is the Sergeant Major, a fear-inducing, high-principled figure, often pictured bellowing relentlessly into the ears of generations of army recruits. He is placed by custom, a history of social engineering and the need for professionalism in combat, at the emotional heart of the military will to serve and fight. While never the commander, the Sergeant Major holds the commanding authority in his office to supervise, enforce and deliver the highest standards of military capability among both officers and private soldiers in order that the commander can achieve his intent.

The feudal system of the Norman kings demanded, in time of need, that tenants of the land must provide the king with rough trained soldiers from the peasantry who were ready to fight. Many of the specific feudal demands placed on tenants in this and other ways were referred to as acts of Sergeanty. This word derived from the ancient French word for 'service' from one who owes allegiance, and that central principle has grown with the word ever since.

An English standing army was formed after the Restoration of Charles II in 1660 and would herald the status of England, and later Great Britain, as a formidable world power. Like all organisations, it needed its own internal management system in order to deliver command effectively to the soldiers in the field. The template for this system was taken from that prevailing in society at the time and the very real differences that existed between the families of power and influence, who generally provided the officers, and those who either had none or less. The latter filled the ranks of soldiers who delivered the Army's punch, and the best of them served by training the others, with the rank of Sergeant. Selected by merit, they marshalled, drilled, equipped and organised men to fight. In 1680 the first use of the term Sergeant Major was applied to the man overseeing a number of Sergeants.

When many regiments or battalions were located close together, they became a garrison, possibly evolving from the French word *garner*, which means 'to equip'. These concentrations were often commanded by Brigadiers or senior Generals and, in London, there was the additional garrison responsibility of protecting the monarch. The first Garrison Sergeant Major London District was appointed in the early 1950s to shape State Ceremonial excellence and always comes from one of the five Foot Guards regiments. Since then there have only been six Garrison Sergeant Majors, each holding office for many years, making them the residual authority on drill. In recognition of the work done by Garrison Sergeant Majors, The Queen approved the revival of the original badge made for Sergeant Majors appointed to the Court of William IV, consisting of the Royal Coat of Arms over four gold chevrons. With an eye for detail shaped from the first step marched by an enlisted Guardsman, this office bearer sets a template that is rigorously applied.

All Queen's Birthday Parade rehearsals on Horse Guards are recorded by the Garrison Sergeant Major's team. His scribe takes notes, and once a page is full, he hands it through a window in Horse Guards where the notes are quickly compiled into an electronic debrief. By the time the Troops have returned to Wellington Barracks and the Guardsmen are changing to board the coaches for the journey home, the officers and Warrant Officers have received an almost immediate debrief in the lecture theatre with printed notes and video footage on a large screen. Both the footage and the notes are sent to the smartphones of all those who have been on parade and in theory they should watch this on their journey back to barracks. No one wants to be seen as the individual who got it wrong and as a result this technology has reduced rehearsal times significantly.

The Garrison Sergeant Major's first Birthday Parade briefing. Represented commanding officers of regiments taking part; the Police; Royal Army Medical Corps; Royal Signals; RAF; Royal Logistics Corps; Army Media; and the BBC.

168   THE ENSIGN

To be chosen as the Ensign to the Escort for The Queen's Birthday Parade is considered a great honour for the young officer selected. With this honour goes the expectation that he is also 'the smartest man on parade', and a highly visible advertisement for his regiment.

The battalion whose Colour is to be trooped that year usually chooses the Ensign from four of its Second Lieutenants, the first rank held on commissioning. While the Escort is picked from the tallest Guardsmen in the battalion, the Ensign hopefuls must endure a 'drill off' under the instruction of the Drill Sergeant and before the discerning eye of the Commanding Officer, who makes the final choice.

Six weeks of relentless training follow for the Ensign elect, with endless repetitions of slow marching, marking time, returning swords and flourishing, until the Ensign's arms grow used to the significant rigours of Colour drill and actions are committed to muscle memory. In a long-standing tradition the previous year's Ensign writes a letter to the current Ensign with sound words of advice and encouragement, thus passing on generations' worth of knowledge. Typical counsel is to try to 'relax and enjoy' the experience, but conquering the nerves of the great occasion can be easier said than done.

One of the key focal moments of the parade is the Flourish of the Colour, when the Ensign lowers the Colour before Her Majesty The Queen, who bows her head in acknowledgement while the Royal Colonels salute. The Ensign needs to show confidence and even a little swagger in this action, so central to the purpose of the parade. The Colour should fall open smoothly as it

As part of the Diamond
Jubilee celebrations in 2012,
The Queen and Prince
Philip dined with all those
who had carried the Colour
of their battalions on the
Birthday Parades of her
reign, at the Cavalry and
Guards Club on Piccadilly.
© Crown Copyright

Lieutenant Ollie Wace,
Grenadier Guards,
lowering the Regimental
Colour for the Royal
Salute. It is usually laid
on the ground, but on
this occasion the ground
was wet.

A long tradition
between Ensigns is
that the previous year's
Ensign writes a letter
to the current Ensign
with words of advice
and encouragement.
Lieutenant Wace is
reading a letter from
Lieutenant Joseph
Dinwiddie, Welsh Guards.

is lowered and all the Battle Honours
be visible, but gusts of wind can hinder
the manoeuvre and cause the Ensign to
lose step. Rain adds significantly to the
weight of the Colour, making it harder
to control both in the Flourish and in
the Recover, when it is returned to the
Ensign's white belt.

However testing the weather
conditions, the Ensign is a focus of
pride for the soldiers who march
behind him, and his own high standards
on parade inevitably make them raise
their game to match and to do honour
to their regiment.

SILVER STICK-IN-WAITING

Colonel Crispin Lockhart portrayed in his appointment as Silver Stick-in-Waiting.

'Gold Stick' and 'Silver Stick' are now purely ceremonial appointments but have ancient chivalric origins. The names unsurprisingly derive from the precious metal heads of the staffs-of-office borne by the titleholders. The unique appointment of Gold Stick-in-Waiting dates back at least to Tudor times when two individuals stayed close to The Sovereign to protect him or her from danger. In 1678 The Sovereign, fearing for his own life, appointed one of three Life Guard Captains to be 'immediately next to the king' and carried 'an ebony staff with a gold head, engraved with His Majesty's cypher and crown'. Later, Gold Stick-in-Waiting was afforded a Deputy (Assistant) in the form of Silver Stick-in-Waiting who could also take up the same bodyguard position in the Royal Household when required. The

Colonel Crispin Lockhart, Lieutenant Colonel Commanding Household Cavalry. Photographed in the Officers' Mess in Knightsbridge Barracks.

roles of Gold Stick-in-Waiting are currently held jointly by the Colonels of The Life Guards and The Blues and Royals – the two Regiments of the Household Cavalry who, as senior in the Household Division and British Army, have always been The Sovereign's personal bodyguard. Currently the appointments of Gold Stick are held by the Colonel of the Life Guards, Lieutenant General Sir Edward Smyth-Osbourne and the Colonel of the Blues and Royals, who is the Princess Royal. The Gold Stick conveys The Sovereign's orders to the Guard and through the authority of the Gold Stick, Silver Stick has the detail of regiments and individuals to carry out royal duties. The Silver Stick-in-Waiting is Lieutenant Colonel Commanding Household Cavalry, holds the rank of Colonel, and has charge of all ceremonial duties for the Sovereign. There are occasions when only Silver Stick is summoned for duty-for example, on the arrival of a head of state on a state visit.

REGIMENTAL CORPORAL MAJOR

'First amongst equals.' At The Queen's Birthday Parade The Life Guards and The Blues and Royals alternate leading the March Past with the Squadron Corporal Major of the appropriate squadron bearing the Sovereign's Standard. The term Corporal Major is a rank unique to the Household Cavalry and is equivalent to the Sergeant Major in other British Army regiments. The reason for the distinction lies with Queen Victoria who dictated that none of her personal bodyguard be referred to as 'Sergeant' as the word derived from 'servant' – a role beneath their status and bearing. The Regimental Corporal Major (RCM) is always a Warrant Officer Class 1 (WO1) in the British Army, a holder of The Queen's Warrant, and the senior Warrant Officer in the regiment. When units have more than one WO1, the RCM is considered 'first amongst equals'. Whenever The Queen is in London throughout the year the daily 'Short Guard' of The Queen's Life Guard at Horse Guards is reinforced with the added protection of an officer, a trumpeter and a Corporal Major bearing the Standard. This is then known as a 'Long Guard'.

Regimental Corporal Major WO2 Salmon, The Blues and Royals, bearing the Sovereign's Standard in the forecourt of Knightbridge Barracks.

DRUM MAJOR'S STAFF COMMANDS

The Drum Major's staff (or mace) began as a functional object for signifying his leading position on the march and to give visible instructions to the drummers and musicians following behind. History has since left its mark on the staff and it has become a tangible symbol of a regiment's unique heritage.

The head of the staff is surmounted by the royal crown and inscribed with the regimental title, badge and devices, while Battle Honours are usually inscribed around the ring on the dome. If there is not enough room on the ring, the scrolls are affixed to the dome. The underside of the head bears the Royal Cypher on one side and the regimental cap badge within the garter, surmounted by the scroll bearing the regiment's name, on the other.

The staff, which measures 5 feet 2 inches, is made of Malacca cane, a very lightweight but strong material known as 'the king of canes'. Metal bands are fixed at intervals around it from which is attached a metal chain. When not in use the staff is placed in a swansdown bag and stored in a purpose-built wooden case.

The MOD's *Drummer's Handbook* of 1985 includes 17 pages of text and illustrations on staff drill for Drum Majors, who must master through determined practice the intricate movements not only to instruct the musicians but also to add panache to the parade.

The Senior Drum Major signalling to other Drum Majors to prepare to halt.

At attention.

The Carry in slow time.

Quick march.

The Trail in quick time.

1st position. Cease playing at the halt.

2nd position. Prepare to cease playing on the march.

The Senior Drum Major preparing to cease playing at the halt.

Members of the King's Troop have mackintoshes to protect rider and horse, but can't wear them on The Queen's Birthday Parade because they have to dismount to fire the Royal Salute.

Throughout the winter months, the Household Cavalry's routine ceremonial duties are conducted in cloaks. In extreme weather, State occasions may also be conducted in this order of dress. The cloak is designed to protect both horse and rider, and used to be carried rolled up on the front of the saddle in summer order. This proved so helpful to maintaining the soldiers' seat in the saddle that a roll of plastic 'packing' is still strapped to the front of the saddle in summer to provide a deep seat. The cuirasses are not worn under the cloak, with a lighter Blues jacket and breeches replacing the heavy tunic and leather breeches. The Household Cavalry still wear capes if rain is forecast for the Parade, but Cape Order for the Foot Guards has been discontinued

R EHEARSALS AND REVIEWS FOR THE BIRTHDAY PARADE The world-famous standards of drill and turnout of the soldiers of the Household Division are a public manifestation of their military qualities: first and foremost, they are fighting soldiers, maintaining the traditions of a unique elite. Their disciplined pride and loyalty as they troop their Colour are forged in years of training, and on battlefields the world over. The immaculate drill they present is the battle drill of an earlier age; it stands not only for pride in their long history of service, but also for their living responsibilities as 21st-century soldiers, masters of an ever-growing range of military skills. The fundamentals – duty, selflessness, discipline, teamwork, loyalty, attention to detail – are ever present; but The Queen's Birthday Parade is also the culmination of meticulous planning, rehearsal and review.

As the parade format is unchanging, rehearsals are in theory simple. However, everyone on parade is acutely aware that Her Majesty has seen this parade more times than anyone else, and knows precisely how it should look. With the vast majority of Household Cavalry soldiers serving at mounted duty for the first two years of their careers before moving on to operational duty, for nearly half of the Troopers on parade this will be their first time. With most never having ridden before joining the regiment, it is a considerable challenge.

The Household Cavalry only has one chance to rehearse on the ground, very early in the morning, before the Major General's Review. The Foot Guards' bands are simulated by Guardsmen with lengths of string, hence this parade is known as 'the String Band'. Rehearsals are mostly in Hyde Park, with troops and squadrons practising the movements in increasingly large groups until ready to move as a division of 25. To wheel a division through 90 degree turns every man must ride an accurate line, adjusting his speed relative to his neighbour to maintain the dressing within the ranks.

Once on Horse Guards the right-hand marker and officer within each division can confirm whether the previously identified window edges, trees, statues and other markers will work for the division. The officer concentrates on judging the pace, to keep the space between the divisions uniform, while the right-hand man of each division judges the line. The centre man keeps the officer, who struggles to see behind him, central to his division.

Endless repositioning would intensely frustrate horses (and men), so precise measuring by the Adjutant and Riding Master ensures that all start in the right place. The Riding Staff ride alongside, directing and making notes for the debrief. Next time will be in front of the Major General, so it needs to be right.

Major Simon Lukas, The Blues and Royals, taking off his boots in the Officers' Mess.

'Eyes right'. The Life Guards ranking past the dais. The right-hand marker keeps his eyes front so that the whole division takes the dressing from him. His eyes are fixed on a window in the Admiralty Building so he rides a straight line.

Lieutenant Colonel
Jerry Levine, Grenadier
Guards, briefing the
ushers who manage the
stands and divert the
spectators, while The
Queen's saluting dais is
being assembled.

The Corps of Drums
march onto the square
via Birdcage Walk.

The Field Officer in
Brigade Waiting, the
Garrison Sergeant Major
and the Drill Sergeant
of the Escort watching
the March On for the
Major General's Review.

Royal Head Coachman Jack Hargreaves giving the Royal Salute as Her Majesty gets onto the dais. For the rehearsal the timings have been written on his glove. Note the digital watch. The Garrison Sergeant Major makes the principals wear these watches, as they can instantly see the time to the second.

The Subaltern officers
reporting to the
Adjutant for the review.

The five bands have
dressed off. The
Senior Drum Major
is ensuring that the
Corps of Drums has
repositioned correctly.

The Garrison Sergeant
Major giving some final
advice to Scots Guards
officers. Their crimson
sash and buff leather
strap to the gold sword
knot are worn when
there is no Royal Colonel
on the Colonel's Review,
and on The Queen's
Guard.

The Major General
Commanding London District
the Household Division

The Garrison Sergeant
Major, Coldstream
Guards, checking
timings

Coldstream Guards
Regimental Sergeant
Major holding The
Queen's Colour with
Battle Honour wreath

Dismounted
Officer, Queen's
Extra Equerry

Irish Guards
drummer with the
Irish Guards mascot

Coldstream
Guards Company
Sergeant Major

Scots Guards
Sergeant

Senior Drum Major

Corps of Drums

Director of Music

Grenadier Guards
musician

Grenadier Guards
musician

Irish Guards piper

Scots Guards Pipe
Major

Household Cavalry
musician

Grenadier
Guardsman
Colour Point

Life Guards Officer

The Blues and
Royals Lance
Corporal with
the Standard

Household
Cavalry
Adjutant

The Blues and
Royals Orderly
Lance Corporal

Scots Guards
Guardsman,
Household
Cavalry Stables

The Blues and Royals
farrier

Household Cavalry
musician

Household Cavalry
drummer

King's Troop
Bombardier Sergeant
with a 13-pounder

Adjutant General's
Corps

Royal Army
Medical Corps
stretcher bearer

Royal Logistics
Corps
photographer

Grenadier
Guardsman
Colour Point

Life Guards Officer

The Blues and
Royals Lance
Corporal with
the Standard

Household
Cavalry
Adjutant

The Blues and
Royals Orderly
Lance Corporal

Scots Guards
Guardsman,
Household
Cavalry Stables

The Blues and Royals
farrier

Household Cavalry
musician

Household Cavalry
drummer

King's Troop
Bombardier Sergeant
with a 13-pounder

Adjutant General's
Corps

Royal Army
Medical Corps
stretcher bearer

Royal Logistics
Corps
photographer

THE BIRTHDAY PARADE The day of The Queen's Birthday Parade dawns very early for most of its participants, human and equine. All must find time to eat a decent breakfast, an essential preparation for the physical exertions ahead (and long, demanding periods of motionless standing at attention). Anyone's worst nightmare is to faint on parade, and on such rare occasions the individual must prove that he or she did indeed eat breakfast or be charged with rendering themselves unfit for duty. By way of further sustenance it is said that some battalions have issued boiled sweets, transferred from hand to mouth surreptitiously during certain movements of arms drill. This may be no more than rumour, but wrappers have been found on the ground after the parade.

Certainly, for those on parade there will be no food between breakfast at about 06:00, and lunch, no earlier than 14:00. In the intervening eight hours, most will have marched at least five miles, bearing a rifle weighing nearly 5kg, in a uniform designed more for impact than comfort. This is why among the earliest to deploy are small parties of medical staff, discreetly positioned to tend to any heat casualties.

Among the first to appear are the Garrison Sergeant Major and his staff, ensuring that the tiny stone squares marking key locations in the ground are in position. Meanwhile, Royal Parks staff meticulously clear any litter, and, in dry conditions, water the gravel to reduce the dust that rises. The Brigade Major will be checking with the Meteorological Office to issue all-important instructions for orders of dress: caped or uncaped.

In the barracks of the King's Troop, the Household Cavalry, the Regimental Bands and the Foot Guards battalions and companies, all those taking part are helping each other to dress, so that uniform and accoutrements are spotless. This takes some hours, until the first troops deploy. Taking their posts early are the signallers who provide the communications which keep the commanders in mutual contact, to adjust timings and speed of marching, and deal with any security issues or unexpected events.

First onto Horse Guards for the parade itself are the Colour Points: chosen NCOs of the Foot Guards bearing the Company Colours to mark the principal turning points. Last off, they have one of the most demanding roles, standing almost motionless throughout. As the crowds gather, other NCOs are selling programmes and distributing any last returned tickets to the lucky few. At the same time the NCOs, Warrant Officers and officers acting as ushers move into position in front of the Standards. Once the half-companies of street liners are in position along the route from Buckingham Palace to Horse Guards, The Queen's Birthday Parade can begin.

06:00
Sergeant Willis, Scots Guards, ironing the Royal Standard on Friday afternoon before the parade.

06:00

*Bulling boots. Pressing.
More bulling. Putting
the final touches to
the Welsh Guards
Regimental Sergeant
Major's tunic. Opposite
page: Attention to detail
– jackboots; shabraques;
buff belts; haircuts.*

*During the evacuation
from Dunkirk in May
1940, a Grenadier
Guards company
marched onto a ship
to be brought back to
England. On the way
they pressed their
trousers and marched
off the ship in true
Guards fashion.*

The first set of ceremonial jackboots the soldiers receive take up to 12 hours to burn, buff and polish to an immaculate finish. Beeswax is applied and a blow torch is used to force the wax into the boot to harden them, then the famous mirror shine is built up with layers of polish, spit and water.

'Off the collar and above the ear.'

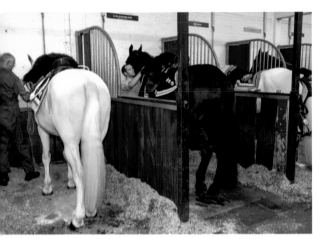

The Chargers being prepared before they are ridden to Buckingham Palace.

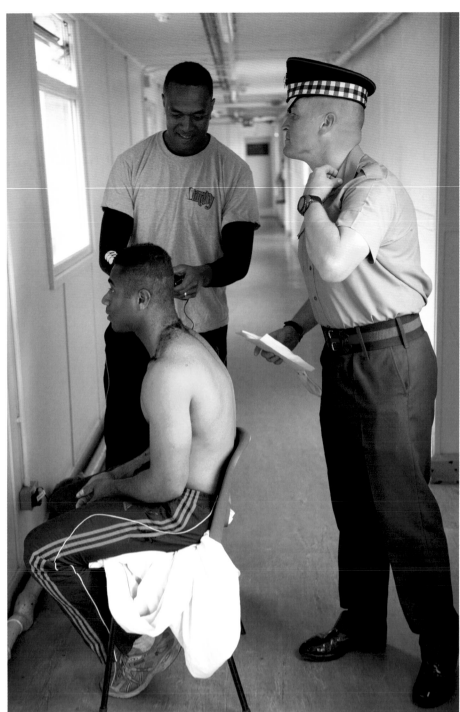

07:00
Lance Corporal Flint, Coldstream Guards, marking a straight line in the gravel in Horse Guards Parade.

Key stone markers engraved with letters are set into the ground and brushed clear of gravel.

10:00
The Colour Points arrive on the Parade Ground.

10:15
The street liners marching into position with Number 3 Band.

It is 1,710 x 30-inch paces from the entrance to Buckingham Palace to the arch of Horse Guards. The Massed Bands march at 30-inch paces and the bass drum is struck at 116 paces per minute, which allows the Garrison Sergeant Major to accurately predict timings for State occasions. He knows that it will take 14 minutes and 45 seconds

for the Massed Bands to arrive at Horse Guards. A similar method, although with slightly different maths, is applied to the precise timing of The Queen's arrival at the saluting dais to ensure that it co-ordinates exactly with the clock chiming at 11:00. The Garrison Sergeant Major takes great pride in achieving this synchronicity.

10:19
The Colour Points march on.

10:29
The escort approach Horse Guards Road.

Subalterns of the
Guards report to
the Adjutant.

10:29
Number 3 Guard form
up on the square.

The Garrison Sergeant
Major gives one of three
signals to the Senior
Drum Major.

10:33
The Colour is marched
on before being uncased
and dressed.

10:30
*The regimental bands
arrive on the square.*

10:35
The Colour is uncased.

10:38
*The Colour Party stands
to attention.*

*The Adjutant rides
onto the parade
ground to form up
the Guards.*

10:38
'Fall in the officers.'

10:39
'Fix bayonets.'

10:54
Presenting arms to members of the Royal Family.

Earl of Wessex,
Honorary Colonel,
London Scots, and the
Countess of Wessex,
Colonel-in-Chief, Corps
of Army Music.

Members of the Royal
Family bow their heads
to the Colours.

10:56
*The Brigade Major salutes
the Colour. His Blues and
Royals retinue are four of the
Troopers who took part in the
Princess Elizabeth Cup. The
winner is on the left.*

10:55
*The dais is put into
position overseen by the
Garrison Sergeant Major.*

10:56
*Her Majesty leaving
Buckingham Palace.*

10:58
*Her Majesty bows her
head to the Colour,
while The Duke of
Edinburgh and the
coachman salute.*

The Queen's Birthday Parade

The Queen inspecting Number 5 Guard.

The Colonel-in-Chief and the Royal Colonels riding behind The Queen during the Inspection. The Duke of Kent always rode a grey because when he was in the Army he served with the Scots Greys cavalry regiment.

The front ranks of the
Massed Bands. The centre
trombone is signalling to the
front rank to counter march.

The parade starts with
the band playing 'Les
Huguenots'. The State Walk
of the Drum Majors.

The Corps of Drums.

The Scots Guards pipers.

The tuba rank.

Drummers' call. After the Massed Bands troop in slow and quick time, one drummer peels away and takes post to the right of the front rank. His drummer's call is the order for the Escort to fall in under command of the Subaltern in preparation for the Trooping.

The Ensign receives The Queen's Colour from the Regimental Sergeant Major in order to troop it through the ranks. He salutes the Colour before returning his sword to its scabbard.

The Ensign grasps the Colour, foots it in the white Colour belt and then about turns to face the Escort.

The Escort for the Colour becomes the Escort to the Colour as the Ensign turns to face Number 1 Guard.

Presenting arms to The Queen's Colour on assuming the role of Escort. The soldiers on the flanks hold their SA80 rifles at the 'high port' to symbolically protect the Colour.

The Massed Bands perform the highly complex spin wheel manoeuvre. This enables the musicians to turn tightly and efficiently in a limited amount of space. There are no drill manual instructions for the movement, merely transmission by word of mouth between generations of Massed Bands.

The Escort re-forms
into line.

The Coldstream Drum
Major looking for the
Garrison Sergeant
Major's signal to
stop playing.

The Queen's Colour
is trooped through
the ranks of the
other Guards by the
Scots Guards.

*Coldstream Guards
marking time in the
March Past while the
Ensign repositions
himself in front of the
Escort in order to lower
The Queen's Colour to
the Sovereign in salute.*

Grenadier Guards
marching past in slow
time. Each soldier must
continuously watch his
dressing to the left, right
and ahead to keep the
lines immaculate.

*Coldstream Guards
marking time.*

*The flourish of the
officer's sword, steps 2,
3 and 4.*

The Recover.

Right flank, 1st Battalion Scots Guards acting as the Escort to The Queen's Colour marching in slow time past The Queen, with the Colour dipped in salute by the Ensign. The band play the regimental slow marches.

Nijmegen Company
Grenadier Guards.

1st Battalion
Welsh Guards.

1st Battalion
Irish Guards.

1st Battalion
Coldstream Guards. The
Colour has a wreath as
the Trooping was on a
Battle Honour day.

The Field Officer in Brigade Waiting gives the command for the Guards to form divisions. On this command, the long and almost unbroken lines of Guardsmen are transformed into a number of evenly spaced company formations.

The Guards then begin to slow march around Horse Guards Parade. Straight lines and precision drill are the order of the day but it takes no small amount of practice to ensure that the correct column distance is maintained.

As the Escort and Guards pass Her Majesty, the music changes to the appropriate slow march of each regiment. Officers salute with their swords, while the other ranks give a sharp 'eyes right'.

The March Past in
slow time.

*Regimental Sergeant
Major, Scots Guards,
with drawn sword –
unique on parade.*

*The Field Officer in
Brigade Waiting rides
to face The Queen after
the March Past in quick
time and salutes his
Colonel-in-Chief.*

*Coldstream Guards in
quick time.*

'Eyes right' in salute
to The Queen during
the March Past in
quick time.

Overleaf: Chaos Corner
is so named because
it appears to be
disorganised. It is, in fact,
a precise construct of
the Drill Manual in order
to deliver each Guard
with the correct gap for
the March Past.

*Forming into the line
at the end of the
March Past.*

The Corps of Drums.

The Massed Bands leaving the saluting line. They left wheel, mark time and halt. The Pipes and Drums play 'Queen Elizabeth'.

In the noise of battle soldiers could see the officer's plume nod as he gave command. This practice continues today on the parade square so that Gunners react immediately to the commands.

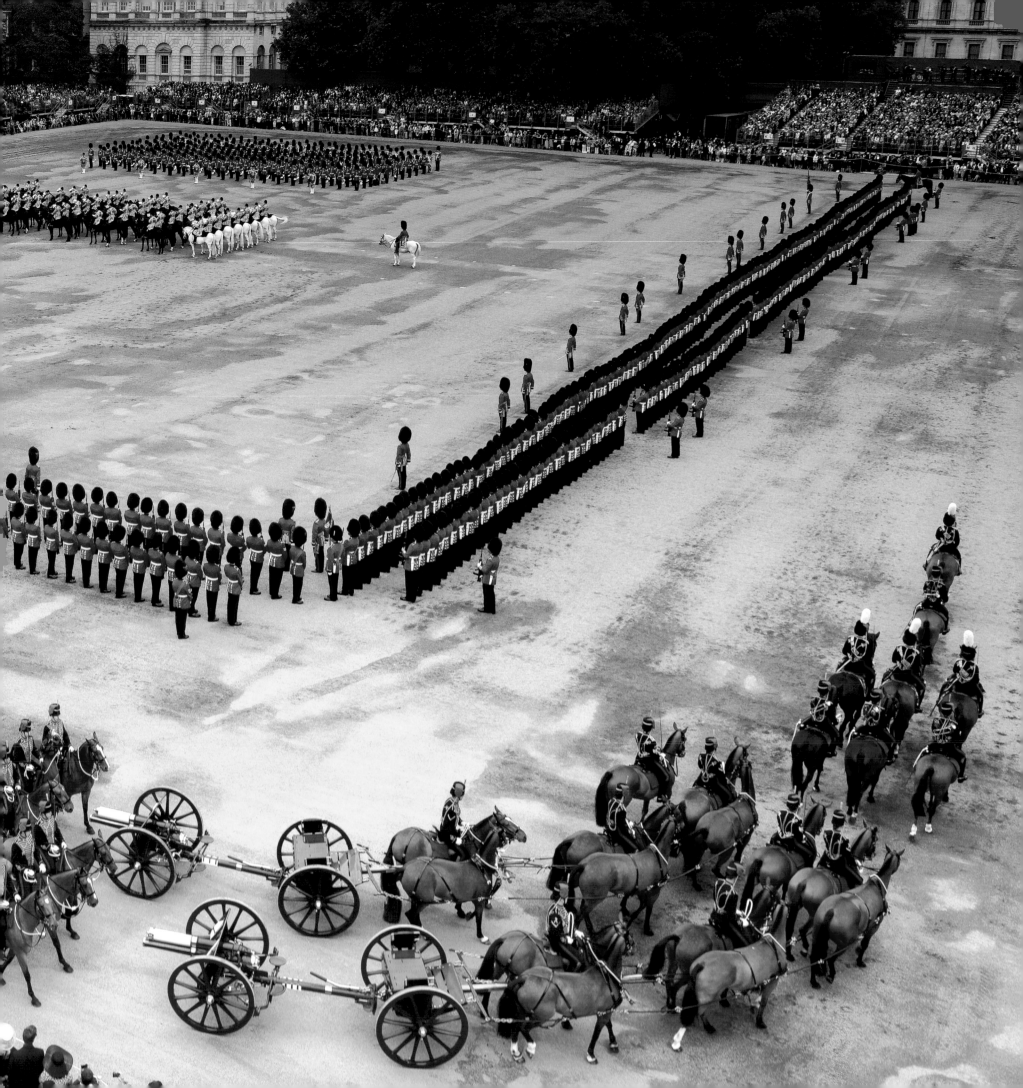

The command to salute
is given by the Number
One (the Sergeant in
charge of the gun).
The drivers and the
detachment smartly
move their head and
eyes to the right. The
drivers also move their
whips, firstly up to their
lips and then hovering
over the withers of their
hand horse as they
march past The Queen
in walk and then trot.

The King's Troop trot past to the 'Grand March' from Verdi's 1871 opera 'Aïda', performed by the Band of the Household Cavalry.

The King's Troop leave the parade ground and wait in Horse Guards Road for the National Anthem and then move to Green Park to prepare for the 41 gun salute at 12:52.

During the rank past in
walk, the officers give
a full 'round arm' Royal
Salute, with the sword
being flourished and
ending beside the boot.
In trot, a 'round arm'
salute is impossible due
to the bouncy nature
of the gait. Instead the
sword pommel remains
lodged on the thigh,
keeping the tip stable,
and an 'eyes right'
is given without
any flourish.

The Squadron Corporal Major dips the Sovereign's Standard in salute at walk.

In trot, only an 'eyes right' is given and the Standard remains in its bucket.

*The dressing is taken
from the right hand
man. He always looks
straight ahead.*

*An 'eyes right' is given in
trot. The spur worn on
the right arm denotes a
riding instructor.*

Once a wheel is complete, the officer signals the end of the turning movement with a 'fly cast' known as 'cutting', bringing the division forward on a straight line.

The farriers, whose black plume in The Life Guards denotes their macabre task in former days, still carry a pole-axe on parade. This immensely heavy item is a reminder of when the spike would be used to put down an irreparably injured horse, and the axe would be used to cut off the near-fore hoof, in which is still carved the horse's number. As with soldiers, every horse has a unique identifying number. Previously, a Quartermaster could use the removed hoof to account for a horse that had been killed in battle. Today, the number ensures that similar-looking black horses are not mixed up – this proved immensely valuable when the barracks had to be evacuated at night in 2011 following a gas leak.

The Farrier Major and his team of around a dozen farriers see their job as helping the horses to have as long a working life as possible. Shoes are tailor-made for each horse, and there is both art and science behind shaping the shoes to correct problems. Good horse sense is a vital quality for the job: being patient and calm, knowing how to read a horse and its mood in order to stay safe in what can be a dangerous situation when holding the hoof of a very large animal.

Aspiring farriers, who will already be enlisted, serve a three-year apprenticeship, learning about equine anatomy and how to diagnose and treat common health complaints alongside acquiring metalwork skills. After six years they complete associate exams to receive a Worshipful Company of Farriers diploma.

The cavalry blacks are Irish Draught crossed with an element of thoroughbred. Historically, as the trumpeter was a crucial enabler for the officer on the battlefield, he rode a grey to be more visible, a tradition that persists.

The traditional crossed sticks salute given by the kettle drummer as the Mounted Bands leave the parade, highlighting that his reins are attached to the stirrups.

The final Birthday Salute to The Queen at the conclusion of the parade. All Guards present arms and the Colour is lowered in obeisance for the last time before being marched to duty with The Queen's Guard at St James's Palace.

The Senior Director of Music conducting the National Anthem.

*The Field Officer
commanding trots
across the square
to salute the
Colonel-in-Chief.*

*'Your Majesty's Guards
are ready to march
off, Ma'am.'*

*He reins back his horse
seven paces, then turns
to face the parade.*

The Garrison Sergeant Major saluting to indicate that Her Majesty is in the carriage and all is clear on The Mall.

On the day of The Queen's Birthday Parade the Honourable Artillery Company fire a 62 gun salute at 13:00 from the Tower of London.
© MoD Crown Copyright.

The King's Troop fire the 41 gun salute in Green Park at 12:52.

The Captain, Subaltern and Ensign of The Queen's Guard are lodged in the Officers' Mess at the heart of St James's Palace. They are responsible for the proper management of the Guardsmen protecting Buckingham Palace and St James's Palace. After the long parade on Horse Guards this duty is their destination, fulfilling the original purpose of the ritual. The Queen's Colour that was trooped is lodged in the corner of the Officers' Mess for safe keeping, and all the Guardsmen know where it is.

From here officers can go to the RAC Club for a swim, taking their swimming trunks in their bearskins.

The Queen's Guard in Colour Court of St James's Palace, immediately in front of the archway of the Gatehouse, beside the old post on which the Colour was once lodged many years ago. With the three officers are the two senior non-commissioned officers.

The grandfather of Captain Wills (second from left) was on duty at the Palace on VE Day, 8 May 1945. He and another officer were summoned by Buckingham Palace to escort the young princesses to the celebrations taking place in front of the Palace gates.

*The Silver Stick Adjutant of the
Household Cavalry and the Regimental
Adjutants of the five Foot Guards
regiments in the Field Marshals' room
in the Cavalry and Guards Club. They
are all wearing the Brigade of Guards
tie. For the Foot Guards, the knot
should be blue, red, blue. For The Life
Guards red, blue. For The Blues and
Royals blue, red. The tie should never
be worn after 6pm or at weddings and
never with a boating jacket!*

THE HOUSEHOLD DIVISION'S determination to maintain the tradition of the annual Queen's Birthday Parade even during the global pandemic of Covid-19 meant that 2020's ceremony was like no other. Not since 1895 has the event taken place at Windsor Castle, but since The Queen moved there in mid-March, earlier than normal for the usual Easter Court, it was decided to hold a reduced Trooping in the Castle Quadrangle, 'behind closed doors'. The pared-back ceremony was performed by 20 members of the 1st Battalion Welsh Guards, which was providing the Windsor Castle Guard. Its small ranks included the first female Guardsman ever to appear on parade for The Queen's birthday.

Ordinarily, Guardsmen would be shoulder-to-shoulder, enabling them to stay in line with one another, but in keeping with government guidelines on social distancing, each Guardsman was tasked with standing 2.2 metres apart, measured by three turns of the pace stick.

Garrison Sergeant Major London District Vern Stokes masterminded the design of the unique ceremony, and oversaw the training, much of which was initially done by virtual means. He said: 'With fewer people on parade there is no hiding place, there never is, and only the highest standard is acceptable, but more spacing between individuals means that there is also no room for errors, and so the soldier has to really concentrate on their own personal drill, reaction to orders, dressing and social distancing.'

The Senior Drum Major leads the band and a company of the 1st Battalion Welsh Guards for the only rehearsal in the Quadrangle. There are usually 13 rehearsals on Horseguards for the Trooping the Colour. For the Windsor celebration they had eight days practice on the grass in Victoria Barracks.

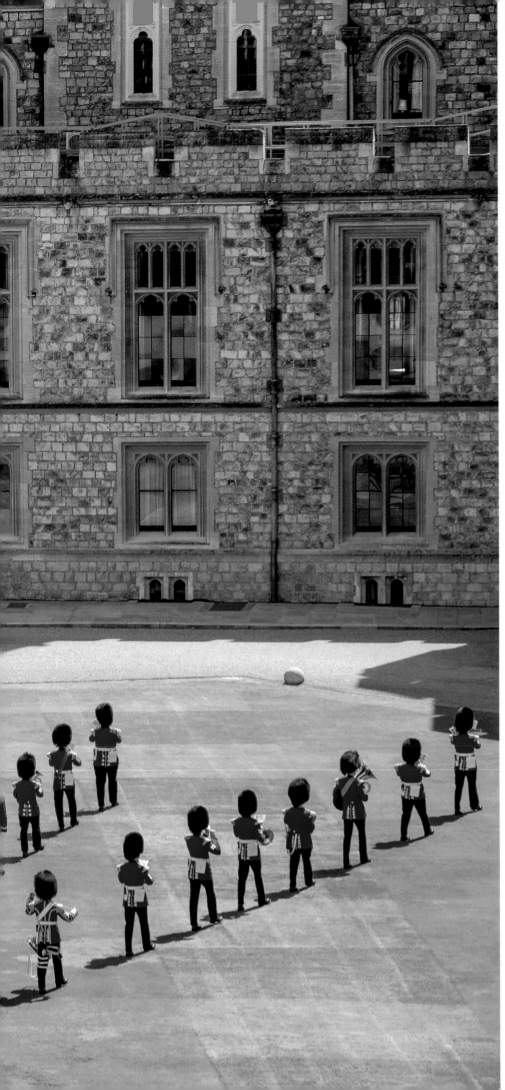

A cohort of 42 musicians from the Massed Bands of the Household Division played a selection of Welsh music during the 20-minute ceremony. A new 'feathering' technique, named for its resemblance to the Prince of Wales's heraldic badge of feathers, was developed to enable the Band to turn 180 degrees while maintaining a safe distance between individuals.

It was still possible to troop the Colour through the ranks by adapting the usual procedure and increasing space between the soldiers. Incorporating the handing over of the Colour by the Regimental Sergeant Major to the Ensign proved more challenging, as the close proximity required would break social distancing guidelines. Instead, the Sergeant Major drew his sword on parade and accompanied the Escort Party as the Colour was trooped, to symbolize his drawing arms to protect the Colour.

Many of the Guardsmen and military musicians who were on parade had, until a few weeks before, been serving on the front line of the national response to the pandemic. In preparation for the delivery of a variety of tasks, soldiers from the Household Division were re-rolled into a Covid Support Force. The Welsh Guards were predominantly involved in the testing programme at regional and mobile testing sites, while the musicians were either on standby to support requests from the civil authorities or to provide Covid-related clerical support to military HQ in London. Immediately following the ceremony, the Windsor Castle Guard returned to the guardroom to resume their guard duty, tradition maintained and history made.

The Band performing a feathering movement in front of Her Majesty. The bass drummer steps to his right so he can see the lead trombonist's signal to about turn given by the Senior Drum Major.

MESS SILVERWARE

Mappin & Webb, Royal Warrant holders since 1897, have produced silver centrepieces, statues and tableware for the Armed Forces for over a century. Many pieces commemorate past battles and hold huge significance for the history of the regiments. The more traditional silver statuettes of soldiers in Tunic Order that they continue to supply to the Guards Division regiments are in Crimea-era uniform, illustrating how keen the regiments are to celebrate their heritage.

However, some of the bespoke silver items now reflect recent conflicts. A Sergeants' Mess might now display a silver statue of a modern-day soldier with the latest GPS and SA80 small arms weapon. Such details will form part of the regiment's history for future generations. While the style of the items has changed over time, the techniques used in their creation have remained mostly the same. The art of silversmithing dates back millennia and all items are still chased by hand.

One recent silver commission came from the 1st Battalion Coldstream Guards. The centrepiece is fondly known as the 'John Amer Pace-sticking Trophy'. Sergeant Amer was tragically killed in Afghanistan's Helmand Province in 2009, and a fitting tribute from the battalion was to commission a piece that reflected something that John loved doing. Indeed, he was part of the Coldstream Guards' team that won the World Championship Pace-sticking Competition at Sandhurst in 2008. The decision was taken that the trophy was to be a pace-sticking team, complete with driver, in action across a drill square. This prestigious trophy is now competed for at the annual Inter Company Pace-sticking Championship.

It will always be a huge privilege for Mappin & Webb to have this unique association with the Household Division as well as many other regiments. It is an honour to help commission sterling silver centrepieces that will outlive all who are involved in their creation. They will simply become beautiful reminders to future generations of those who served before them.

Her Majesty the Queen riding Burmese.

John Amer Pace-sticking Trophy.

The Household Cavalry
Standard Bearer.

The Drum Major of the
Household Division.

Senior Drum Major
Household Division
Queen's Birthday Parade

One of six Guardsmen
on which the Regimental
Sergeant Majors have
their names inscribed.
There is also one for
the Garrison Sergeant
Major.

PRESENTED BY MAPPIN & WEBB

Regimental Grenadier
Guards Sergeant
Major with the Colour.

Coldstream Guards
Ensign with the Colour.

The King's Troop, Royal
Horse Artillery.

THE ROYAL PARKS

The Park Manager of St James's Park and Green Park Mark Wasilewski and his team of staff and contractors are stage managers for The Queen's Birthday Parade. Their preparations begin some time before with the planting of 13,000 red geraniums in front of Buckingham Palace to match the Guardsmen's tunics. From early morning on the day itself the gravel of the undulating ground of Horse Guards Parade has been raked and graded to ensure a uniform appearance. If the forecast is dry, water is then sprayed by bowser onto the gravel to prevent dust from being kicked

up by hooves onto the guests. In hot weather evaporation can occur rapidly, and Mark remains on the edge of the parade ground ready to signal for the bowser to depart as soon as he hears the first approaching band.

In the early hours all road islands and traffic lights have been removed to provide the complete width of The Mall for the procession that leads The Queen between Buckingham Palace and Horse Guards Parade. Sand is spread at key points to ensure that those horses pulling carriages and field guns do not slip. The Green Park gardeners will have trimmed branches and cut the grass to the

correct length for the King's Troop to ride in and fire the 41 gun salute.

The Mall is never swept so many times in a single day as it is for the day of the parade. It must be spotless for Her Majesty's departure from the Palace, and once that journey is completed the operation is repeated for the homeward procession. Once the parade is over and the troops dispersed, Mark leads the road sweepers back one final time to clear all remaining horse muck, prior to the public being allowed onto The Mall for the balcony appearance by The Queen and members of the Royal Family and then the flypast.

From left to right:

Greg Brown
Ed Hosten
Mo Miah
Paul Hosten
Chris Worsley
Wilfred Sappleton
Mark Wasilewski
Malcolm Kerr
Alison McAtamney
Will Tremorin
Alex Kirby
Peter Chioba

Designed and typeset by Jennifer Penny and Prof. Phil Cleaver of et al design consultants (www.etal-design.com)

Tamsin Shelton, freelance editor

Susan Coulthard, Senior Media Officer. Army Communications. HQ London District, Horse Guards, Whitehall

Garrison Sergeant Major Vern Stokes, Coldstream Guards

Captain PJR Chishick, Life Guards, Adjutant HCMR

Captain Nico Wills

Garrison Sergeant Major William Mott, Welsh Guards

Regimental Corporal Major Peter Ireland, HCMR

WO2 (Regimental Quartermaster Sergeant) Mark Cox, Grenadier Guards

Carl Bailey of Mappin & Webb

Senior Drum Major Scott Fitzgerald, Coldstream Guards

Senior Drum Major Damian Thomas, Grenadier Guards

Picture credits
Page 12 Bridgeman Images
Credit: Mounting Guard (coloured engraving), Rowlandson, T. (1756–1827) & Pugin, A.C. (1762–1832) (after) / Private Collection / © Look and Learn / Elgar Collection
Page 18 Bridgeman Images
Credit: King George II (1683–1760) at the Battle of Dettingen, with the Duke of Cumberland and Robert, 4th Earl of Holderness, 27th June 1743, c.1743 (oil on canvas), Wootton, John (1682–1765) / National Army Museum, London / Acquired with assistance of National Art Collections Fund
Page 22 Bridgeman Images
Credit: Trooping the Colours on the Horse-Guards' Parade in Honour of the Queen's Sixty-Eighth Birthday (engraving), English School (19th century) / Private Collection / © Look and Learn / Illustrated Papers Collection
Page 26 Press Association
Credit: © AP/PA

Picture preparation by Joe Thomas (www.joe-digital.com)

Thanks to all of the below, and to those I have forgotten, my apologies. Colin Dean, for his musical knowledge of the Household Division. Lt. Col. Wayne Hopla. Mr Charles Heath-Saunders SO2 Media Projects. Major Andrew Chatburn SO2 Ceremonial. Major Robert Skeggs CO The King's Troop. Capt. Claire Blakiston Adj. The King's Troop. Capt. M.D.de.B. Wilmot RHG/D. Capt. George R.J. Ashby LG. Capt. Will Tulloch SG. Capt. Joseph Dinwiddie WG. Capt. Hugo Coddrington CG. Pipe Major Ross McCrondle SG. WO2 RQMS John Gavin IG. Cpl. Major O'Dell HCMR Officers' Mess. Cpl. of Horse Dan Short HCMR. Staff Sgt. Rupert Frere. Sgt. Darren Hardy CGBand. Sgt. Allen The King's Troop. LSgt. Strudwick CG. Sgt. Flower Wellington Barracks.

Julian Calder MStJ

There are two key elements to Trooping the Colour: the Sovereign and The Queen's Colour of the selected Foot Guards battalion. For the first time ever, this portrait brings together a monarch with all eight extant Queen's Colours, flanked by the two Sovereign's Standards of the Household Cavalry Mounted Regiment.

Opposite: Close up of the baldric, the Senior Drum Major's State Dress.

Julian Calder, Mark Pigott and Alastair Bruce would like to thank Her Majesty The Queen, His Royal Highness The Duke of Edinburgh for his generous foreword. His Royal Highness The Duke of York and His Royal Highness The Duke of Kent for graciously consenting to having their portraits taken for this book.

A project such as this requires busy people to go that extra mile so our thanks to the Major General, the Chief of Staff, the Brigade Major and all at Horse Guards for their welcome and unwavering support for, and belief in, this project. Thanks also to Helen Cross and Paul Whybrew. To all the staff at Wellington, Knightsbridge and Woolwich Barracks for their help and enthusiasm and to Media Ops for always responding favourably to my frequent badgering.

Also to all the writers (four Generals!), Colonel Dan Hughes, Andrew Wallis of The Guards Museum, Martin Westwood of The Household Cavalry Museum, David Cowdery of The Cavalry and Guards Club, Lieutenant Colonel Dowell Conning, Padre of The Guards Chapel. Also to Andrew Manley for his knowledge of the Birthday Parade. Finally to all the Officers, Warrant and Non-Commissioned Officers, Gunners, Troopers and Guardsmen who agreed to be photographed.

A handful of the photographs in this book are not mine, so thanks to Sergeant Rupert Frere, Sergeant Adrian Harlen, Sergeant Paul Randell, Sergeant Donald Todd, Adrian Myers, Bob Martin, Tom Lovelock and Nick Johns for the use of their pictures.

This has been a long project, involving many early mornings and late nights. Thanks to my wife and to my sons for their support, and apologies for the occasions when I have sounded a bit like a Sergeant Major.

My late father-in-law, General Sir Charles Harington, was an inspiration. He decided early on in life that he would always strive to be the best he could at everything he did.

Julian Calder MStJ

A CIP catalogue record for this book is available from the British Library

ISBN 978.0.9553253.7.3

Printed and bound in China by Artron Art (Group) Co., Ltd.

Text copyright © Julian Calder Publishing 2020
Photographs copyright © Julian Calder 2020
(www.juliancalder.com)

Design and layout copyright © Julian Calder Publishing 2020

Top row:

A Colour Sergeant holding a marker flag.
The proof mark and stamp on a sword.
London District tactical recognition flash.
The head kit of the Scots Guards
Colonel's charger.
The muzzle of the 13-pound King's
Troop gun.
The Ensign cleaning the Grenadier Guards
motif on the sling.
A Grenadier officer standing at ease.

Second row:

The King's Troop Commanding Officer's
despatch pouch.
The rose motif on the shoulder of a
Coldstream Guards Sergeant.
A Welsh Guards Warrant Officer's
belt buckle.
The Corps of Army Music tactical
recognition flash.
The end of the Gold Stick.
The end of a Household Cavalry Riding
Staff's whip.
A company badge on the camp flag of the
Grenadier Guards.

Third row:

The Brigade of Guards tactical
recognition flash.
The star on the plaque on Wellington
Barracks Square.
A Trooper of the Household Cavalry holding
his sword.
The Coat of Arms on the back of the
chair from which Her Majesty reviews
the parade.
A senior Guards officer mounted on
a rehearsal.
The Garrison Sergeant Major's arm badge
of rank.
An officer's SAS wings.

Fourth row:

Farriers' tactical recognition flash.
The saddlecloth of the Colonel,
Scots Guards.
The Blues and Royals eagle.
The Grand Duke of Luxembourg's Irish
Piper's banner.
The staff of the Sergeant Major, 2nd
Battalion Grenadier Guards.
The numbered hooves of a Life
Guards horse.
The Riding Staff of the King's Troop arm
badge of rank.